Sanrio
HELLO KITTY®

Forever Cute, Creative & Collectible
Anita Yasuda

Schiffer Publishing Ltd

4880 Lower Valley Road, Atglen, PA 19310 USA

© KidKraft® Inc.

Designed by John P. Cheek
Cover design by Bruce Waters

Type set in Freehand 591 BT/Souvenir Lt BT
ISBN: 0-7643-2352-0
Printed in China
1 2 3 4

Published by Schiffer Publishing Ltd.
4880 Lower Valley Road
Atglen, PA 19310
Phone: (610) 593-1777; Fax: (610) 593-2002
E-mail: Info@schifferbooks.com

For the largest selection of fine reference books on this and related subjects, please visit our web site at **www.schifferbooks.com**
We are always looking for people to write books on new and related subjects. If you have an idea for a book please contact us at the above address.

This book may be purchased from the publisher.
Include $3.95 for shipping.
Please try your bookstore first.
You may write for a free catalog.

In Europe, Schiffer books are distributed by
Bushwood Books
6 Marksbury Ave.
Kew Gardens
Surrey TW9 4JF England
Phone: 44 (0) 20 8392-8585; Fax: 44 (0) 20 8392-9876
E-mail: info@bushwoodbooks.co.uk
Free postage in the U.K., Europe; air mail at cost.

Kitty Kontents

Acknowledgments

I would like to thank the following companies for all their help and enthusiasm for this project: Sanrio offices in both Japan and the US, Hello Kitty licensees for sharing their great products, Paul Frank Industries Inc., Hollywood Digital for the fabulous Kitty Ex. brand collaborations, and of course, all of Kitty's friends who shared their collections from large to small.

May all your days be filled with happy thoughts.

Let's Love Hello Kitty Today, Tomorrow & Always.

© Blue Box Toys ™

Chapter One
Hello! I'm Kitty 🌸

Kitty Quotes ~ "I'm Kitty and I'm here to brighten your
day with my warm heart and fun-loving ways!"

Coin Purse. A reproduction of the first product ever made. A star is born! 1975.

Hello! My name is Kitty White, a.k.a. Hello Kitty! I was born November 1, 1974 in England.

I live with my Mama, Papa, and sister Mimi in a little brick home with a cheerful red roof in a suburb of London. Perhaps you have seen pictures of it on a bag, letterbox, or key chain? 'Togetherness brings happiness' is the motto around the White home. If you have never been to England, you must come.

I have apple trees in my garden. And as many of you know, I weigh as much as three apples. In the spring the first buds appear followed by gorgeous white flowers. Mimi and I love to sit in the cool shade of the trees in summer and have tea. I love a tea party! Grandma often makes us a pudding and Grandpa comes over and paints.

The apples ripen and in the Autumn they are ready to pick. You must come and help me pick some. Apple pie is Mama's speciality.

One of my special shy friends lives in the garden. Can you guess which one? Yes, Mory of course. He doesn't help pick the apples but he does enjoy watching us. Perhaps if you come over, he will poke his head out just for you!

Another wonderful thing about my home is the lane in front. So many people walk past our home daily. There's my friend Joey who is great at sports. Fifi, she's quite chatty at school and is in the third form. Tippy is brilliant and Mimi and I like to ride our bikes with him to the ice cream store.

On school mornings, Mimi and I get picked up by a red mini bus. I blow a kiss up to my window for Tiny Chum, the best Teddy in all of England. 💕

I sit beside my friend Cathy or Tracy but he is always up to mischief. Mama thinks it best not to sit next to him. On the drive to school I often see my other friends, Rory, Tim, and Tammy, in the trees.

Yes, school is most exciting because we go on many excursions. At the amusement park I conducted a marching band, rode on a roller coaster, and had a ride on an elephant!

I belong to the Tennis Club. A sweet little penguin is my partner. Other sports I enjoy are sailing, windsurfing, and roller-skating. I am the only girl to have a pilot's license in third form!

During my holidays I love to travel. I make frequent trips to Japan, which is my second home. My family has homes in Puroland and Harmonyland. My house was just remodelled in honour of my birthday. You will think it ever so cute.

In Japan I see my picture everywhere; from marshmallow packages to purses. Why, there was even a postcard with Cathy and I in Kyoto, and one of us up in Hokkaido! I have quite the postcard collection.

I love to write and send cards to my friends. Email is super convenient but I like looking in the post and seeing an envelope with my name on it. *To: Miss Kitty White.* It makes me so happy!

We haven't decided where our next holiday will be but my friend Yuko Yamaguchi has a few good ideas.

I am the happiest littlest girl in the whole world because I have such good friends like you. 💕

I hope to see you soon. Have a fine day!
Hugs, Kitty XOXO

Chapter Two

Kistory ❀

Kitty Quotes ~ "Feelin' Fine In The Summer Sunshine" 1999

The following twenty-five cards are part of a 25th Anniversary commemorative postcard set produced in 1999. (*The date in the following captions refers to the design year.*)

~1974~

Kitty in her now classic seated pose created by Yuko Shimizu. Kitty 's birthday is November 1st, making her a Scorpio.

~ Memorable Saying ~
I like drawing.

~ Kitty Trivia ~
(Q) The first design includes which two objects on either side of Kitty ?
(A) A fish bowl and a glass of milk. Source: coin purse 1976

~1975~

The first product called a 'petite purse' is produced. After the purse is released Hello Kitty 's name is decided upon. The key figures in Kitty 's life are

introduced as well: Papa George White, Mama Mary White, and Mimmy, Kitty 's twin.

~ Memorable Saying ~
Togetherness Brings Happiness.

~ Memorable Moment ~
The Strawberry News begins. The first issue costs 100 yen.

~1976~

Even though it is only the 2nd year of the collection, Hello Kitty is very popular in Japan. A variety of Hello Kitty electric and wooden goods from counting toys to trains are on the shelves.

~ Memorable Saying ~
Happiness Is...

~ Memorable Moment ~
Sanrio begins to license

Kitty's likeness and exports begin. In 2004 there were 600 domestic and 300 licensing companies abroad.

~1977~

The first standing pose is created by Kitty 's second designer, Setsuko Yonekubo. Kitty launches into a series of new and exciting activities such as piloting a plane. Stationary is still great but with the new Kitty fashion goods line fans can emulate an older sibling.

~ Memorable Saying ~
I'm so glad I'm a country girl.

~ Kitty Trivia ~
(Q) How much is Kitty 's bow shown as costing on designs from the 70s?
(A) $1.25. Source: paper 1977

~ Memorable Moment ~
Kitty releases her first record, aptly named *That Child Is Kitty.*

~1978~

Kitty becomes more active. We see her flying planes and sailing on a yacht thanks to the marine sports boom in Japan.

~ Memorable Saying ~
Honk the honker…drive carefully.

~ Trivia ~
(Q) Can you name one object which is appliquéd onto Kitty 's overalls in 1978?
(A) An elephant, an anchor, or a train. Source: glass, plush 1978

~Memorable Moment ~
Yuko Yamaguchi becomes Kitty's third designer.

~1979~

A variety of goods from ski hats to dishes, and letter sets to aprons are introduced. For the first time Kitty is seen riding on an elephant.

~ Memorable Saying ~
It's a lovely day.

~ Trivia ~
(Q) What is often shown sitting atop the school roof?
(A) A small yellow or white bird. Source: mail box 1979

~ Memorable Moment ~
Grandpa White and Grandma White make their debut.

~1980~

A surge of interest in tennis in late 1970s Japan sees Kitty wearing a t-shirt emblazoned with the logo 'I love tennis'. From the 1980s a shift in color and design begins with a definite preference for the color red. Yuko Yamaguchi's piano design appears in *The Strawberry Times*. Her design was not turned into any products.

~ Memorable Saying ~
Viva Summer.

~ Trivia ~
(Q) What book is Kitty often shown reading?
(A) Fairy Tale. Source: tissue package 1980

~ Memorable Moment ~
A digital watch released this year becomes a million dollar seller.

~1981~

More unique poses that feature Kitty holding a variety of objects, raising one hand to say hello, and facing forward are introduced. A big effort to cultivate fans across genders and generations is made. One such example is the basketball hoop for male fans. Of course we know now that girls can jump too!! Go Kitty Go Kitty Go Kitty !!

~ Memorable Saying ~
Summer of blue skies.

~ Memorable Product ~
The rotary dial telephone and camera are introduced.

~Memorable Moment ~
The first Kitty animated movie is released.

~1982~

The Kitty and Tiny Chum series begins with Tiny Chum featuring more prominently in designs. This change reflects the popularity of Teddy Bears in Japan. Other changes include no black outline on some graphics and more grownup Kitty images.

~ Memorable Saying ~
Smile for me.

~ Trivia ~
(Q) Who is shown driving the school bus?
(A) Kitty. Source: pillow 1982

~ Memorable Moment ~
Kitty picture & coloring books are published by Random House USA.

~ Memorable Product ~
A Kitty hairdryer.

~1983~

Kitty is so happy with Tiny Chum that she is shown in many poses holding him up or with him seated on her lap. She is also shown sipping a mug of hot chocolate with the word 'Pleasantime' in the design. To Japanese ears *Pleasantime* evokes images of foreign destinations.

~ Memorable Saying ~
What's new?

~ Trivia ~
(Q)What club is Kitty a member of this year?
(A) Kitty 's marine sports club. Source: bottle holder 1983

~ Memorable Moment ~
Kitty is chosen as the Children's Ambassador for UNICEF.

~1984~

Kitty has an even broader array of activities planned this year. Not just stationary anymore, we even see Kitty windsurfing.

~ Memorable Saying ~
Let's learn to count.

~Memorable Moment ~
The still photo series is launched.

Hello Kitty

~1985~

A new country series is launched. Kitty appears in checks, long skirts and even apron dresses. Perhaps Yuko Yamaguchi's visit to the States influenced the design.

~ Memorable Saying ~
Kitty 's best home cooking, it's a special day

~ Trivia ~
(Q) What kind of pie does Kitty bake on the country series?
(A) A chocolate cream pie. Source: sketchbook 1985

~ Memorable Moment ~
Designs were specifically aimed at high school students.

~1986~

A series which only shows Kitty 's face debuts and is soon a favorite among fans. Other goods continue to show her from head to toe, wearing clothes in style with current trends such as polka dots and flare skirts.

~ Memorable Saying ~
I love my teddy bear.

~ Trivia ~
(Q) What does Kitty ask if you will be free for in 1986?
(A) A cup of tea. Source: vinyl bag 1986

~1987~

The monotone series in black and white is extremely successful among high school girls and young women. No matter how Kitty is shown, she is always charming.

~ Memorable Saying ~
What's up?

~ Trivia ~
(Q) What vegetable is shown on Kitty 's watering can?
(A) A carrot. Source: watering can 1987

~ Memorable Product ~
A solid gold medallion is put on the market.

~1988~

The tartan check design reflecting Kitty 's British heritage and the Andy Warhol-inspired Kitty pattern are prominent. The clothing series launches with items such as rain ponchos to under garments.

~ Memorable Saying ~
Did you cuddle your teddy bear today?

~ Trivia ~
(Q) In Kitty 's home what objects does Tiny Chum's image appear on?
(A) A chair, alarm clock, and umbrella, etc. Source: handkerchief 1988

~ Memorable Moment ~
CBS broadcasts the animated program *Hello Kitty 's Fairy Tale Theatre*. It was produced in the USA.

~1989~

A cute series modeled after popular American comics uses exciting color combinations on a variety of goods.

~ Memorable Saying ~
Good times are for sharing with friends.

~ Trivia ~
(Q) In the Kitty comic series Mama is making breakfast. What does she make?
(A) A Western style breakfast including sausages, eggs, toast and coffee. Source: notebook 1989

~ Memorable Product ~
A limited Hello Kitty television is released to mark the 30th anniversary of the founding of Sanrio.

~1990~

Many varieties of Kitty are seen: polka dot, mono-tone, and primary color series.

~ Memorable Saying ~
I love a tea party.

~ Trivia ~
(Q) Whose image is on Kitty 's teapot?
(A) Teddy. Source: a *noren* 1990

~ Memorable Moment ~
Sanrio Puroland amusement park opens in Tama City.

~1991~

A flower series using a spectrum of pastel colors creates a new look. Many unique products such as the Kitty walkie-talkies are released.

~ Memorable Saying ~
This is a good day 'cause I'm with you.

~ Trivia ~
(Q) On which side is Kitty most likely to be holding her Teddy?
(A) On the left. Source: pouch, pencil case 1991

~ Memorable Moment ~
Sanrio Harmonyland amusement park opens in Oita Prefecture.

~1992~
Since her birth Kitty has had many image changes. This year is the culmination of romantic and feminine designs. Cherries and hibiscus flowers set the tone for this colorful series.

~ Memorable Saying ~
Pretty as a posy...cheerful as gingham.

~ Trivia ~
(Q) What small hand instruments were seen this year?
(A) Maracas and a castanet. Source: hand-held rhythm makers 1992

~ Memorable Moment ~
A Southeast Asian Hello Kitty musical performance begins.

~1993~
Through imaginative design changes Kitty establishes herself as trend setter.

~ Memorable Moment ~
The animated television program *I Love Hello Kitty* starts broadcasting on TV Tokyo. It is still broadcast under a new name, *Kitty Paradise Fresh*.

~ Memorable Character ~
Baby Hello Kitty and Daniel are introduced.

~1994~
Hello Kitty's trademark bow changes to a flower. More goods just like Mom's are introduced with an emphasis on functionality and fun, such as the Kitty palm pilot or cellular phone.

~ Memorable Saying ~
Friends make dreams come true.

~ Trivia ~
(Q) What kind of fiesta did Kitty hold this year?
(A) A fruit fiesta. Source: tote 1994

~ Memorable Moment ~
UNICEF Japan appoints Hello Kitty as their goodwill envoy.

~ Memorable Product ~
The first Hello Kitty cellular phone.

~1995~
The nurse series is a huge hit and introduces new colors to the classic red design line with the introduction of Kitty in pale blue and even sunflowers in pink.

~ Memorable Saying ~
Good Health Starts with Cleanliness.

~ Trivia ~
(Q) What language other than English or Japanese is seen on Hello Kitty goods?
(A) French. Source: notebook 1992

~ Memorable Moment ~
Sanrio's family musical begins nationwide performances in Japan.

~1996~
Hello Kitty face and flower series combines a herringbone pink check, flowers, hearts, and Kitty's face. Popular with fans is the commencement of the Hello Kitty Print Club. In Japan special Hello Kitty photo booths are set up, where visitors are able to choose Kitty decorations to add to their photos.

~ Memorable Saying ~
Summer's ripe for fun.
Trivia ~ (Q) On which side does Kitty wear her ribbon or flower?
(A) The left. Source: camera, bag, cup, etc.

~ Memorable Moment ~
Hello Kitty *ningyoaki*, or bean cakes, are sold at Tokyo Station marking the beginning of the regional Kitty goods series. By 2004 there are 450 regional designs.

~ Memorable Milestone ~
The first brand specifically for adults called Vivitix debuts in Shibuya, Tokyo Sanrio store.

~1997~
Three rosebuds replace Kitty's classic ribbon. This design debuts in the October 5th *The Strawberry Times*, No. 357. Hello Kitty goods for everything, from cosmetic bags to small games, are on the market.

~ Memorable Product ~
A quilted cellular phone case in pink.

~ Memorable Moment ~
The Kabuki series is developed.

~1998~
A year with many technological firsts such as a Kitty personal computer. The Yamaha Motor Co., Ltd. Hello Kitty scooter and the Daihatsu Kogyo Co., Ltd. small car

hit the streets of Tokyo. Even a bankbook and credit card from the Dai-ichi Kangyo bank sport Kitty's image.

~ Memorable Moment ~
Dai-ichi Kosho, one of the largest karaoke equipment manufacturers, opens a Kitty karaoke room. Kitty's house opens in Sanrio Puroland.

~ Memorable Mail ~
NTT (Nippon telegraph and telephone company) begins a Hello Kitty promotion featuring a plush Kitty doll with each telegram sent.

~1999~
Kitty and the white Pegasus design is used on bags to towels and clothing to teacups. The pale blue and white series is fresh and young.

~ Memorable Moment ~
Dear Daniel merchandise is introduced and he begins appearing as Kitty's boyfriend at Puroland and Harmonyland.

~ Trivia ~
(Q) What '70s Hello Kitty scene was revisited this year?
(A) The ice cream shop scene with Kitty and Mimi on a tricycle. Source: handkerchief 1976

~2000~
Many stylish goods such as glasses and even a wine bottle opener featuring romantic designs are made available for the mature fan.

~ Memorable Moment ~
Amon Miyamoto produces a musical review of Hello Kitty featuring Hello Kitty's signature theme song in Sanrio Puroland.

~ Trivia ~
(Q) Who is most likely to be angel alongside Kitty this year?
(A) Cathy. Source: postcard 2000

~2001~
The stylish graffiti line in pink and black is used on items from teddies to purses. Your pink kitchen is now complete with the Kitty sandwich maker and mixer.

~ Memorable Moment ~
Sanrio opens its first Japanese style store in Ikebukuro, Tokyo.

~ Trivia ~
(Q) Who was wearing a wedding dress this year?
(A) Kitty of course! Source: plush doll 2001

~ Memorable First ~
The Heavens Sono Hara Ski Resort reopens in Nagano as a Hello Kitty ski center and is very successful.

~2002~
This card celebrates Kitty's 28th birthday. During her 28th year The Café Goods series is a huge hit. The design uses a simple bulls eye with the words 'Café de Kitty' inside.

~ Memorable Saying ~
Think positive.

~ Trivia ~
(Q) What instrument are Kitty & Daniel shown playing on the Aloha Goods.
(A) A ukulele. Source: plastic bag 2002

~ Memorable Moment ~
Kitty and Tweety co-brand goods are sold exclusively in Asia, and the New York design team Heatherette shows it's Hello Kitty collection in New York.

~ Memorable Music ~
The Kitty record *Koishichina Town/Mou Nakanaiyou* is released by Zomba Records Japan.

~2003~
Kitty fairy is as popular as ever, but a sleek line using the KT logo really stands out. The area surrounding Puroland known as Tama Center is made-over with help from Sanrio friends and is known as the place where you can see Hello Kitty. Signage now uses Hello Kitty's likeness as well as other Sanrio characters.

~ Memorable Collaboration ~
The Kitty Taxi begins service in Kanagawa Prefecture.

~ Memorable Moment ~
Kitty The World is broadcast on BS Fuji television from May to October.

~2004~
Around 300 commemorative items are available including the limited ribbon and angel series. Kitty's likeness is seen on stamps as well as coin sets from the mint bureau of Japan.

~ Memorable Saying ~
30 years of cute.

~ Kitty Trivia ~
(Q) What is the most expensive product ever made with Kitty's likeness?
(A) Queen Kitty. A platinum figurine encrusted with diamonds; worth 10 million yen and sold by Mitsukoshi. The least expensive items are marshmallow and rice cracker snacks for 20 yen. Source: Sanrio Co. Ltd.

~Memorable New Friend ~
Kitty's pet kitten and hamster are introduced through a series called Charmikitti.

~ Memorable Moment ~
Hello Kitty is named UNICEF Special Friend of Children.

Chapter Three

A Gift From The Heart ✿

Kitty Quotes ~ "I'm So Glad I'm A Country Girl" 1977

SUBJECT: shopping
FROM: fifi@preciousmiss.uk
TO: kitty@threeapples.uk
DATE: 28 July, 5:00PM

Dear Kitty,
     I have just come from the first Japanese style Hello Kitty store in Ikebukuro. It opened in 2001. Too cute! My purchase was wrapped beautifully. A small premium was placed on top and secured with an adorable sticker. I will carefully place it in my suitcase and show you when I return.
     See you soon. Say hi to everyone back home.

Sayonara, Fifi

SUBJECT: shopping
FROM: kitty@threeapples.uk
TO: fifi@preciousmiss.uk
DATE: 29 July, 9:00AM

Hi Fifi,
     Sounds fun. Mimi and I will definitely put it on our 'to do' list for our next visit to Japan. We are off to the countryside to visit our Uncle's farm today. Mimi is such a homebody but I managed to convince her to come. I'm so glad I'm a country girl!

Hugs, Kitty ✿
P.S. Mimi says hi

Sticker Set. $10-15, 1976.

Mini-Pocket Mirror. $3-5, 1997.

Stamp. $3-5, 1997.

Paper Holder. Kitty reads a book entitled *Fairy Tale*. $10-15, 1977.

The word thank you is written in *katakana* lettering.

Pillow Ornament. $3-5, 1995.

Stamp. $1-3, 1997.

Kitty Tales ~ After the 1970s, premiums became more colorful and versatile.

The underside of the stamp reveals Kitty and Tiny Chum cheek to cheek. In *katakana* lettering is written the word kiss.

Hand Castanet. $1-3, 1997.

Maraca. $1-3, 1997.

T-Shirt Ornament.
$1-3, 1997.

©'76,'97 SANRIO
TOKYO, JAPAN

©'76,'97 SANRIO
TOKYO, JAPAN
MADE IN CHINA

Hello Kitty

Medallion.
$1, 1997.

Tiny Tops With
Roulette Pattern.
$1-3, 1997.

Kitty Tales ~ During the nineties, premiums were more than just simple ornaments—they became detailed objects which could be played with.

Finger Puppet.
$1-3, 1997.

Finger Puppet.
$1-3, 1998.

Yellow Eraser.
$1-3, 1998.

Red Drawstring Bag. $1-3, 1998.

Pink Ring. $1, 1999.

©'76, '99 SANRIO
TOKYO, JAPAN

13

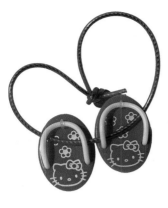

Red *Geta*.
$1, 1999.

Spiral Bound Notebook.
$1, 1999.

Wall Hangers.
$1, 2000.

Kitty Figurines.
$2-5, 2000.

Noise Maker. $2-5,
2000.

Kaleidoscope.
$2-5, 2001.

Red Hairbrush.
$1, 2000.

Push Locks.
$1-3, 2001.

Jewelry Tray. Made
especially for the Hello
Kitty 's 25th Anniversary. It
was a gift to readers of *The
Strawberry News*. $2-5,
2000.

Kitty Face Castanet.
$1, 2001.

Pinball Game.
$1-3, 2000.

Handheld Pinball.
$1-3, 2001.

Bookmark.
$1, 2001.

Pinball Fortune
Game. $2-5,
2003.

Blue Suitcase.
$1-3, 2003.

View Finder.
$1-3, 2001.

Hologram.
$1, 2004.

Reverse View Of Hologram.

Christmas Ornament.
$1-3, 2002.

30th Anniversary Box. Each box
contained either Hello Kitty or a
member of her family. $2-5, 2004.

Compact Mirror.
$1-3, 2002.

Papa White Figurine.
$1-3, 2004.

Chapter Four
Creative Kitty ❀

Kitty Quotes ~ "I Like drawing" 1976

SUBJECT: school
FROM: kitty@threeapples.uk
TO: daniel@shallwedance.uk
DATE: 3 September, 9:00AM

Dear Daniel,
Can you believe that a new term starts at school tomorrow? Mama has pressed my clothes and Papa is lending a hand to make lunches. Mimi wants to ride tricycles to school but Mama said no. Break is over...sigh. I luv school, I wonder what new things we shall learn? I can't wait to hear all about your travels to Africa and New York. Bring your pictures.
See you on the bus.
Kitty ❀

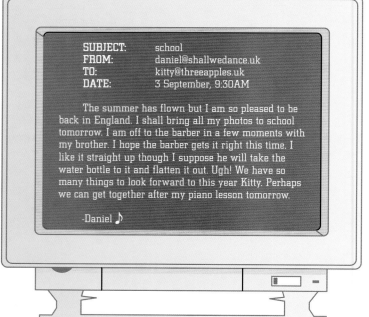

SUBJECT: school
FROM: daniel@shallwedance.uk
TO: kitty@threeapples.uk
DATE: 3 September, 9:30AM

The summer has flown but I am so pleased to be back in England. I shall bring all my photos to school tomorrow. I am off to the barber in a few moments with my brother. I hope the barber gets it right this time. I like it straight up though I suppose he will take the water bottle to it and flatten it out. Ugh! We have so many things to look forward to this year Kitty. Perhaps we can get together after my piano lesson tomorrow.

-Daniel ♪

Let's take a peek inside Kitty's school bag...

Origami. $15-20, 1976.

Letter Pad. $15-20, 1975.
Courtesy of Sanrio Co. Ltd.

Pencil Holder. $25-30, 1975.
Courtesy of Sanrio Co. Ltd.

Mini Ruler Set. $25-30, 1976.
Courtesy of Sanrio Co. Ltd.

White Metric Ruler. $10-15, 1976.

Puffy Stickers.
$10-15, 1976.

Japan Air Lines® Pencil Box. The five red
pencils have been cleverly decorated to look like
Hina Matsuri dolls. $20-25, 1987.

School Bus Pencil Case. $30-35,
1977. *Courtesy of Sanrio Co.
Ltd.*

Christmas
Origami. $5-10,
1988.

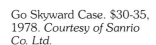

Notepad In Fan Design.
$5-10, 1997. *Courtesy
of Sanrio Co. Ltd.*

Go Skyward Case. $30-35,
1978. *Courtesy of Sanrio
Co. Ltd.*

GREET THE SUN WITH A BIG HELLO

GO SKYWARD!

Pencil Leads.
$2-5, 1998.

Days Of Fun Notebook.
$20-25, 1979. *Courtesy of
Sanrio Co. Ltd.*

Stamp Set. $1-3, 1998.

Harmonyland Notebook.
$2-5, 1999.

Small Coloring Book.
$1-3, 2000.

Large Orange Decal.
$2-5, 1999.

Sticker Book.
$2-5, 2000.

Blue Coloring
Book. $1-3,
2000.

Pencil Lead Sticks.
$1-3, 2000.

Mini Tape Dispenser. $1-3, 2001.

Pink Coloring Book.
$1-3, 2000.

Kitty Tape Refills.
$2-5, 2001.

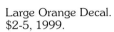

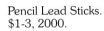

19

Reusable Seal Book.
$1-3, 2001.

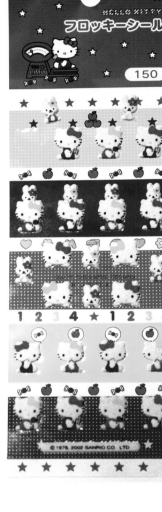

Sticker Sheet.
$1-3, 2002.

Origami Paper.
$2-5, 2002.

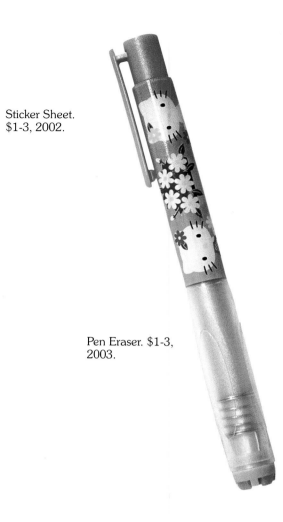

Pen Eraser. $1-3,
2003.

Dolphin Kitty Ball Pen. $1-3, 2002.

Pencil Case. $2-5, 2003.

Notebook. $2, 2004.

Me & My Diary.
$2-5, 2003.

Glue Stick. $1, 2004.

Kitty's desk is always cool!

Teeter-Totter Stapler. $10, 2004. *Courtesy of Takara® USA Corp.*

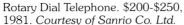

Rotary Dial Telephone. $200-$250, 1981. *Courtesy of Sanrio Co. Ltd.*

HELLO KITTY

Rainbow Carousel Pencil Holder. $15, 2004. *Courtesy of Takara® USA Corp.*

HELLO KITTY

Solar Calculator. $20-25, 1989. *Courtesy of Sanrio Co. Ltd.*

Windmill Pencil Sharpener. $15, 2004. *Courtesy of Takara® USA Corp.*

Sticky Patch Swing Set. A glue stick is hidden in the log. $10, 2004. *Courtesy of Takara® USA Corp.*

Solar Powered Kitty. $10, 2005. *Courtesy of Tomy® Corporation*

Catch-A-Clip Pond. $10, 2004. *Courtesy of Takara® USA Corp.*

Chapter Five

Kitty Correspondence ✿

Kitty Quotes ~ "Summer Of Blue Skies" 1981

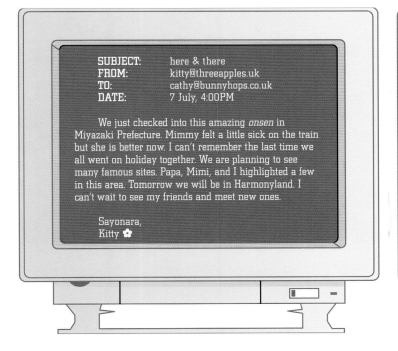

SUBJECT: here & there
FROM: kitty@threeapples.uk
TO: cathy@bunnyhops.co.uk
DATE: 7 July, 4:00PM

We just checked into this amazing *onsen* in Miyazaki Prefecture. Mimmy felt a little sick on the train but she is better now. I can't remember the last time we all went on holiday together. We are planning to see many famous sites. Papa, Mimi, and I highlighted a few in this area. Tomorrow we will be in Harmonyland. I can't wait to see my friends and meet new ones.

Sayonara,
Kitty ✿

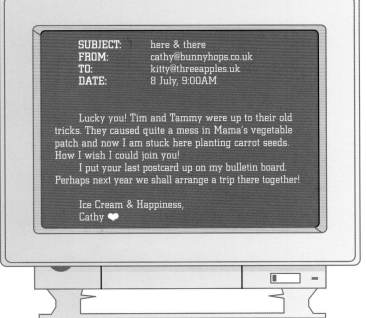

SUBJECT: here & there
FROM: cathy@bunnyhops.co.uk
TO: kitty@threeapples.uk
DATE: 8 July, 9:00AM

Lucky you! Tim and Tammy were up to their old tricks. They caused quite a mess in Mama's vegetable patch and now I am stuck here planting carrot seeds. How I wish I could join you!
I put your last postcard up on my bulletin board. Perhaps next year we shall arrange a trip there together!

Ice Cream & Happiness,
Cathy ❤

Envelope. Kitty and Mimi ride their tricycles to the store. $5-8, 1976. *Courtesy of Sanrio Co. Ltd.*

Envelope. Kitty -The-Pussycat. $5-8, 1975. *Courtesy of Sanrio Co. Ltd.*

Pouch. Exclusively sold at Japanese postal outlets. $10, 2004.

Strawberry Paper Set. $5, 2003.

Envelope. What beautiful music! From the Hello Kitty Best Collections Package. $1, 2004.

Kitty and Mimmy Atop A Dolphin. $1, 2000.

Envelope. Hello Kitty Best Collections Package. The classic 1976 rollercoaster scene comes to life again. $1, 2004.

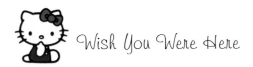

Wish You Were Here

Red, Blue & White Kitty. $1, 2000.

Kitty & Cathy Among The Daisies. $1, 1999.

Kitty 's Changing Looks. $1, 2000.

Promotional Postcard.
$1, 2003.

Kitty Fairy and Cathy.
$1, 2003.

Bellbottom Jeans Kitty. $1, 2003.

Kitty dressed in an old fashioned smock and dress enjoys a day at the seashore. $1, 2004.

Kitty Face Design.
$1, 2004.

Regional Series Postcard. Kitty Hokkaido with magical pastel stars in the winter sky. $1, 2004.

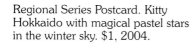

Kitty dressed as an official Japanese letter carrier. $1, 2004.

A retro 1970s inspired design with Kitty and a variety of signature objects interspersed between the letters of the alphabet. $1, 2004.

Kitty and Mimmy are off on a tricycle ride through the tulips. The images were also used on a handkerchief design from 1976. $1, 2004.

Countryside Kitty Postcard Set. These four cards all depict Kitty in various lush pastoral settings. $4 for set. 2004.

Kitty in a sea of pink daisies. This postcard was part of a set sold by the Japanese postal system $1, 2004.

Chapter Six

Peek~A~Boo! A Hanky For You ✿

Kitty Quotes ~ "What A Cheerful Gingham Day!" 1987

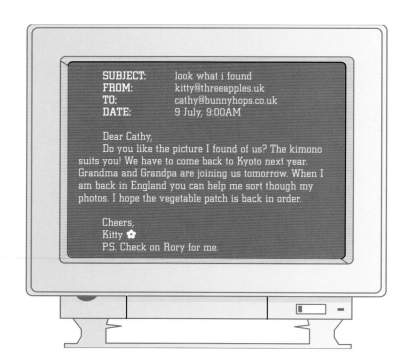

SUBJECT: look what i found
FROM: kitty@threeapples.uk
TO: cathy@bunnyhops.co.uk
DATE: 9 July, 9:00AM

Dear Cathy,
Do you like the picture I found of us? The kimono suits you! We have to come back to Kyoto next year. Grandma and Grandpa are joining us tomorrow. When I am back in England you can help me sort though my photos. I hope the vegetable patch is back in order.

Cheers,
Kitty ✿
P.S. Check on Rory for me.

Ice Cream Brings Happiness.
$25-30, 11" x 11", 1975.

Kitty & Mimi
On Tricycles.

Kitty 's Room Is Full Of Fun And
Play! $20-25, 11" x 11", 1976.

Kitty Grows Tomatoes. $25-30, 11" x 11", 1976.

Look At All The Fun Things!
$20-25, 8" x 8", 1976.

Hello Kitty Standing Pose.
$20-25, 11" x 11", 1976.

Hello Kitty Time Schedule.
$20-25, 11" x 11", 1976.

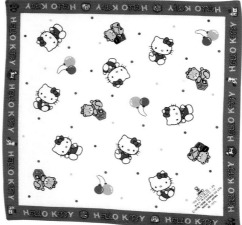

Kitty Action Poses. $5-10,
11" x 11", 1986.

Peek A Boo! I See You! Let's
Play Hide-And-Seek! $20-25,
11" x 11", 1976.

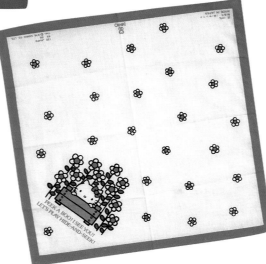

A Cup of Tea Always
Tastes Good. $10-15, 11"
x 11", 1988.

Something Good's Sure To Come Your Way. $10-15, 11" x 11", 1988.

Patterned Hearts & Cuddles. $5-10, 11" x 11", 1997.

Hello! Lovely To Meet You! I'm Kitty. $10-15, 11" x 11", 1989.

Red And White Check. $5-10, 12" x 12", 1998.

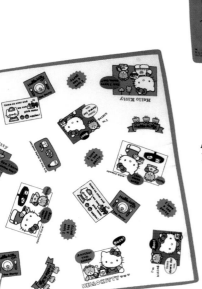

A Tea Party. $10-15, 11" x 11", 1990.

Red Polka Dot Design. $5-10, 10" x 10", 1999.

25th Anniversary. $15-20, 12" x 12", 1999.

Kitty And Apples. $5-10, 12" x 12", 2000.

The amusement park. This scene is based on a 1976 tin candy box design. $5-10, 12" x 12", 2001.

 Take-Out Kitty

The Pilots. $5-10, 7" x 7", 2002.

Take Out Lunch. $5-10, 7" x 7", 2002.

Pizza Delivery. $5-10, 11" x 11", 2002.

Chapter Seven

Girl Next Door 🌼

Kitty Quotes ~ "Go Skyward!" 1978

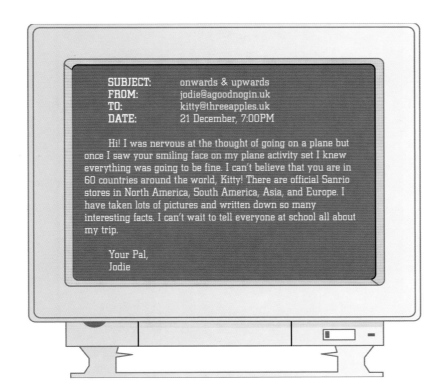

SUBJECT: onwards & upwards
FROM: jodie@agoodnogin.uk
TO: kitty@threeapples.uk
DATE: 21 December, 7:00PM

Hi! I was nervous at the thought of going on a plane but once I saw your smiling face on my plane activity set I knew everything was going to be fine. I can't believe that you are in 60 countries around the world, Kitty! There are official Sanrio stores in North America, South America, Asia, and Europe. I have taken lots of pictures and written down so many interesting facts. I can't wait to tell everyone at school all about my trip.

Your Pal,
Jodie

Mount Fuji. Kitty and Cathy outfitted in mountaineering gear prepared to scale Mount Fuji. $10, 8" x 8", 2000.

Osaka. *Osaka, Kitty Story* is written at the bottom of the handkerchief in *kanji* and the word *Naniwa* (regional slang for Osaka in *katakana* on the banner). $10, 8" x 8", 2000.

Nara. Cathy offers Kitty, who is dressed up as a Nara deer, a biscuit. $10, 8" x 8", 2000.

Kyoto. Kitty and Cathy dressed in kimonos take in the famed cherry blossoms at the *Kinkakuji* in Kyoto. $10, 8" x 8", 2001.

Kitty Tales ~ Deer are considered to be messengers of the gods in the Shinto *religion and Nara's deer have been designated a National Treasure.*

Hamanako. Kitty is dressed as one of the famous eels from Hamanako in Shizuoka. The large blue *hiragana* character is the letter "u" as in *unagi*; the Japanese word for eel. $10-15, 8" x 8", 2001.

Kyoto. In the distance, an image of Kitty is emblazoned on the mount for the *Daimonjiyaki* festival. The traditional *hanko* reads Hello Kitty in the bottom left hand corner. The famous *Toji* pagoda, the largest in Japan, is also shown. $10, 8" x 8", 2000.

Nigata. Kitty and Cathy, dressed in *yuki mino*, make their way through the snow. Kitty is singing a classic children's winter song "*yuki ya kon kon*" or "the snow is steadily coming down." $10-15, 8" x 8", 2002.

Wakamatsu. Kitty, Kathy, Tippy, and Fifi are dressed as *byakkotai*. They are standing in front of the Aizu Wakamatsu *Tsurugajo* Castle. $10-15, 8" x 8", 2001.

Shimizu. Kitty is poised at the head of a wooden fishing boat in Shimizu, Shizoka. The flags indicate to the people waiting on shore *tairyo*, or a great fishing day was had. $10-15, 8" x 8", 2002.

Kanazawa. Kitty visits the main attraction in Kanazawa, the famous *Kenrokuen* garden. $10-15, 8" x 8", 2002.

Furano. Kitty with Cathy in the famed lavender fields of Furano, Hokkaido. $10-15, 8" x 8", 2002.

Iga. Dressed as ninjas from Iga in Mie Prefecture, where a style of ninja originated. $10-15, 8" x 8", 2002.

Nagano. Kitty is busy harvesting radishes. The large *kanji* in the upper right corner reads *hidaji*. It refers to a famous mountain route through the Japanese Alps in Nagano Prefecture. $10-15, 8" x 8", 2002.

Kitty and Cathy are dressed as *Shinsengumi*, private guards of the Emperor. A very popular story, *manga* and movies surround this elite guard. The flag reads *Makoto*, which means faithful, as in faithful to the emperor. $10-15, 8" x 8", 2002.

Nagasaki-iki. Kitty is dressed up as the famous demon of Nagasaki-iki. There is a cliff with an unusual rock formation here, which according to local legend was created by a demon's footstep. $10-15, 8" x 8", 2002.

Kamaishi. Kitty, Cathy and Bear are dressed as tigers for the Kamaishi Tora Mai festival. The tiger dance is one of the traditional folk arts in this area. This festival is designated a national treasure. $10-15, 8" x 8", 2003.

Mount Fuji. Kitty and Cathy travel along the famous *Tokkaido* route. $5-10, 8" x 8", no date.

Wajima. Kitty and Cathy are at the famous morning market in Wajima. Their wares displayed in baskets with small signs in *hiragana*. $10-15, 8" x 8", 2003.

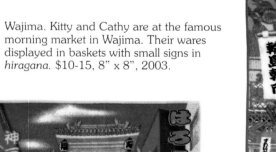

 Such A Lucky Girl

Kobe. The two friends stand in front of the gates to Chinatown in Kobe. Cathy holds up a tray of *gyoza* and Kitty shows off the Chinese *manju*. $10-15, 8" x 8", 2003.

Good-Luck Charms. The regional Kitty series encompasses a wide range of merchandise from handkerchiefs to charms, plush dolls etc. Hello Kitty dressed as a tiger. $1, 1999. The larger *omamori* is from Miyaji-jima in Kyushu. $3, 1997.

Chapter Eight

Cute as a Button ✿

Kitty Quotes ~ "I Am A True Fan Of Fun Loving People" 1985

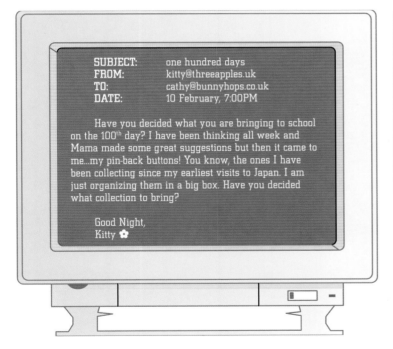

SUBJECT: one hundred days
FROM: kitty@threeapples.uk
TO: cathy@bunnyhops.co.uk
DATE: 10 February, 7:00PM

Have you decided what you are bringing to school on the 100th day? I have been thinking all week and Mama made some great suggestions but then it came to me...my pin-back buttons! You know, the ones I have been collecting since my earliest visits to Japan. I am just organizing them in a big box. Have you decided what collection to bring?

Good Night,
Kitty ✿

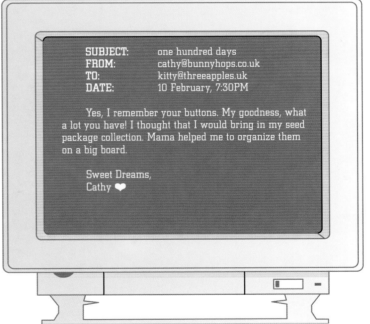

SUBJECT: one hundred days
FROM: cathy@bunnyhops.co.uk
TO: kitty@threeapples.uk
DATE: 10 February, 7:30PM

Yes, I remember your buttons. My goodness, what a lot you have! I thought that I would bring in my seed package collection. Mama helped me to organize them on a big board.

Sweet Dreams,
Cathy ♥

Kitty Amongst The Flowers. $1, 1996.

Diamonds & Hearts. $1, 1996.

Dressed For Winter. $1, 1999.

Kitty 's Face. $1, 1997.

Red & White Checks. $1, 1997.

Snow Princess. $1, 2000.

Fairy Kitty &Tiny Chum. $1, 2000.

Blossom Kitty. $1, 2000.

Rainbow Kitty & Cathy. $1, 2000.

Mermaid Kitty & Cathy. $1, 2000.

Night Sky Fairy Kitty. $1, 2000.

25th Anniversary Of Kitty

The following fifteen badges were all manufactured in 1999. They are part of a set produced for the 25th Anniversary of Hello Kitty. Each badge represents a specific design of that year. The complete set: $15.

1974 Design Year.	1978 Design Year.	1981 Design Year.	1986 Design Year.	1993 Design Year.
1975 Design Year.	1979 Design Year.	1982 Design Year.	1989 Design Year.	1995 Design Year.
1976 Design Year.	1980 Design Year.	1984 Design Year.	1992 Design Year.	1998 Design Year.

The Chinese Calendar With Kitty & Sanrio Friends

The following eight badges were manufactured in 1999. They are part of a twelve-piece set. The entire set: $10.

Year of The Dragon. Characteristics: Popular and full of life. Famous Dragons are Nyago and Robowan.

Year of The Ox. Characteristics: Born leaders, inspire confidence.

Year of The Tiger. Characteristics: Bold and adventurous. Famous Tigers are Hello Kitty, Patty & Jimmy, and Coro Coro Kuririn.

Year of The Snake. Characteristics: Romantic, wise, and charming. Famous Snakes are Pochacco, Pekkle, Sweet Coron, and U.S.A. HA.NA.

Year of The Rooster. Characteristics: Hard working. Famous Roosters are Picke Bicke, Badtz Maru, and Pippo.

Year of The Rabbit. Characteristics: Affectionate and lots of friends. Famous Rabbits are My Melody, Keroppi, Pink no Corisu, and Landry.

Year of The Dog. Characteristics: Honest and faithful.

Year of The Boar. Characteristics: Honest and tolerant.

Chapter Nine

Fun & Play ✿

Kitty Quotes ~ "It's Nice To Play in The Sun With Your Friends" 1980

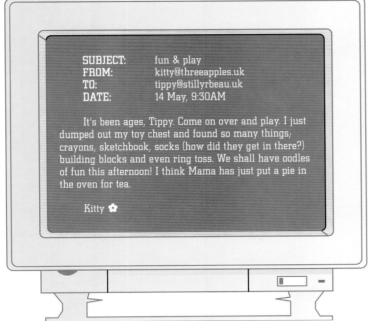

SUBJECT: fun & play
FROM: kitty@threeapples.uk
TO: tippy@stillyrbeau.uk
DATE: 14 May, 9:30AM

It's been ages, Tippy. Come on over and play. I just dumped out my toy chest and found so many things; crayons, sketchbook, socks (how did they get in there?) building blocks and even ring toss. We shall have oodles of fun this afternoon! I think Mama has just put a pie in the oven for tea.

Kitty ✿

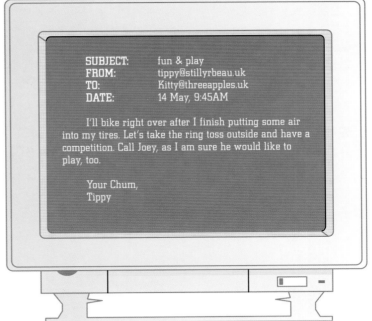

SUBJECT: fun & play
FROM: tippy@stillyrbeau.uk
TO: Kitty@threeapples.uk
DATE: 14 May, 9:45AM

I'll bike right over after I finish putting some air into my tires. Let's take the ring toss outside and have a competition. Call Joey, as I am sure he would like to play, too.

Your Chum,
Tippy

Light Up Crystal Castle. A unicorn, swan, and carriage create a magical castle. $20, 2000. *Courtesy of Blue Box Toys*™

Candy Store. Kitty, Tracy, and Cathy have dropped in for a treat. $20, 2000. *Courtesy of Blue Box Toys*™

Carry Along Mini Dollhouse. Living room, bathroom, and bedroom furniture all included. $10, 2000. *Courtesy of Blue Box Toys*™

Victorian Doll House Play Set. $20, 2000. *Courtesy of Blue Box Toys*™

Light Up Dream House. Fully furnished, it even sports skylights, a pool, and lawn furniture. $20, 2000. *Courtesy of Blue Box Toys*™

Hello Kitty Roller Disco. A mirrored ball and rental roller skates make this a happening place for Kitty and friends. $20, 2000. *Courtesy of Blue Box Toys*™

Snowman Hello Kitty. $10, 2002. *Courtesy of Bandai® America Incorporated. ©1976, 2004 Sanrio Co. Ltd.*

Flower Fairy Hello Kitty. $10, 2002. *Courtesy of Bandai® America Incorporated. ©1976, 2004 Sanrio Co. Ltd.*

Woodpecker Hello Kitty & Woodpecker Wagon. $10-15, 2002. *Courtesy of Bandai® America Incorporated. ©1976, 2004 Sanrio Co. Ltd.*

Mermaid Hello Kitty & Shell Hotel. $10-15, 2002. *Courtesy of Bandai® America Incorporated. ©1976, 2004 Sanrio Co. Ltd.*

Confection Hello Kitty & Sweet Shoppe. $10-15, 2002. *Courtesy of Bandai® America Incorporated. ©1976, 2004 Sanrio Co. Ltd.*

Hello Kitty Deluxe Play Set. Nutty Tree with Squirrel Hello Kitty and Mimmy. $20, 2002. *Courtesy of Bandai® America Incorporated. ©1976, 2004 Sanrio Co. Ltd.*

Deluxe Kitty's House. The two-story house came with a 2.5" flocked Hello Kitty small doll and included a detailed TV and VCR, room lights, appliance set, and a vacuum cleaner. $50, 2002. *Courtesy of Bandai® America Incorporated. ©1976, 2004 Sanrio Co. Ltd.*

Puzzle. Kitty and Mimmy's class-room. $10, 1999.

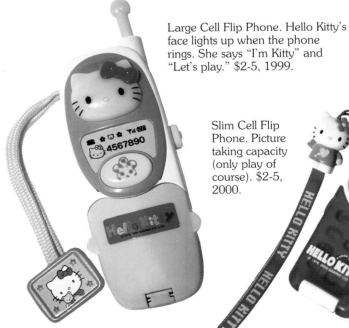

Large Cell Flip Phone. Hello Kitty's face lights up when the phone rings. She says "I'm Kitty" and "Let's play." $2-5, 1999.

Slim Cell Flip Phone. Picture taking capacity (only play of course). $2-5, 2000.

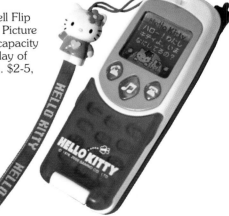

Mini Car. Floral details take this Bug back in time. $5-10, 2000.

Hello Kitty Cassette Karaoke. $20, 2000. *Courtesy of Blue Box Toys*™

Hanestuki. A traditional Japanese New Year's game played with a wooden paddle called a *hagoita* and a shuttle called a *hane.* $10, 2002.

Electronic Scan n' Count. $20, 2000. *Courtesy of Blue Box Toys*™

Sticker & Card Maker. Sticker tape, cards, and paper will make your correspondence fun. $20, 2000. *Courtesy of Blue Box Toys*™

Memory Maker. A fuzzy pink Memory Book, colored pencils, gel pens and markers, stickers stamps, and more. $15, 2004. *Courtesy of JAKKS Pacific, Inc.*

Kitty Ballerina Latch Hook Mat. $10, 2004. *Courtesy of JAKKS Pacific, Inc.*

Activity Traveller. $10, 2004. *Courtesy of Giddy Up, LLC*

Game Book. $10, 2004. *Courtesy of Giddy Up, LLC*

Scratch & Design. $10, 2005. *Courtesy of Giddy Up, LLC*

Hello Kitty
MicroPets. 30th
Anniversary
Limited
Collector's
Edition. $8,
2004. *Courtesy
of Tomy®
Corporation*

Professor Rubik's® Cube
Hello Kitty. Kitty herself
turns and twists to make
an amazing puzzle. Around
150,000 were sold! $20,
1999. *Courtesy of Seven
Towns Ltd.*

Pink Etch A Sketch®. $15, 2003. *Courtesy of Sababa Toys*™

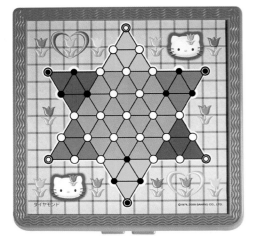

Portable Game Chest. Featured six different magnetic game boards. $10, 2000.

Etch A Sketch®. Doubles as a cool purse to store your stuff! $15, 2003. *Courtesy of Sababa Toys*™

Dominoes. The friendly faces of Kitty and friends match up instead of dots. $15-20, 2003. *Courtesy of Sababa Toys*™

Tin Lunch-Box Style Case. $10-15, 2003. *Courtesy of Sababa Toys*™

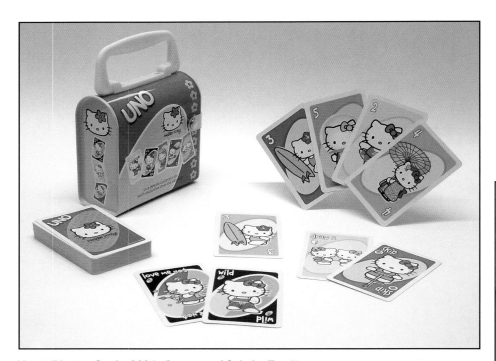

Uno® Playing Cards. 2004. *Courtesy of Sababa Toys™*

Hello Kitty Themed Chess Board. $35, 2004. *Courtesy of Sababa Toys™*

Uno® Carrying Tin. 2004. *Courtesy of Sababa Toys™*

Chapter Ten

Brave & Bold ~ Good To Hold

Kitty Quotes ~ "I Love My Teddy" 1986

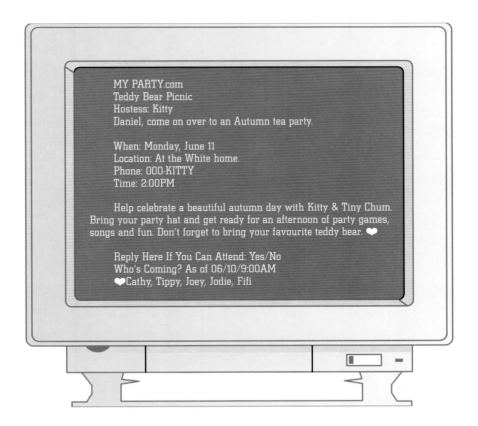

MY PARTY.com
Teddy Bear Picnic
Hostess: Kitty
Daniel, come on over to an Autumn tea party.

When: Monday, June 11
Location: At the White home.
Phone: 000-KITTY
Time: 2:00PM

Help celebrate a beautiful autumn day with Kitty & Tiny Chum.
Bring your party hat and get ready for an afternoon of party games,
songs and fun. Don't forget to bring your favourite teddy bear. ❤

Reply Here If You Can Attend: Yes/No
Who's Coming? As of 06/10/9:00AM
❤Cathy, Tippy, Joey, Jodie, Fifi

Hello Kitty Angel. $5-10, 1998.

Pajama Kitty. $5, 2002.

Kitty & Mimmy Plush.
$5-10, 1998.

Fairy Plush. $5, 2002.

Bunny. $5, 1998.

Flower Fairy Plush. Available at postal outlets in Japan. $20-25, 2004.

Halloween Hello Kitty Plush. $10, 2004. *Courtesy of Nakajima® USA, Inc.*

Japanese Clip-Ons & Plush. Three different kimono designs. $10, 2004. *Courtesy of Nakajima® USA, Inc.*

Ballerinas & Romeo and Juliet. $10, 2004. *Courtesy of Nakajima® USA, Inc.*

Hello Kitty Attitude Clip-Ons & Plush. $10, 2004. *Courtesy of Nakajima® USA, Inc.*

Scooter Kitty. $10, 2005. *Courtesy of Nakajima® USA, Inc.*

Rose Garden Playhouse. A portable home with a bumblebee Kitty. Three other designs were also produced; seashell, ice cream cone & mushroom. $15, 2005. *Courtesy of Nakajima® USA, Inc.*

Stick-On Decoration. $5, 2005. *Courtesy of Nakajima® USA, Inc.*

Kitty Heart Angel. $10, 2005. *Courtesy of Nakajima® USA, Inc.*

Chapter Eleven

Kitty Karry~Alls 🌸

Kitty Quotes ~ "Pleasantime" 1984

Dear Grandma and Grandpa,
We are having a wonderful holiday. We all miss you. Especially me! I can't wait to see all the paintings Grandpa has made while I have been away. I have used the beach bag and my rucksack for carrying all the sand toys to the beach. This afternoon we are going windsurfing! How exciting! Papa promises to take lots of snaps.

XOXO, Kitty
P.S: Remember to feed my fish

Small Turquoise Coin
Purse. $20-25, 1976.

HELLO KITTY

Bus/Train Pass Case.
$20-25, 1976.

"I Love My Grandparents" Canvas
Bag. $30-35, 1976. *Courtesy of
Sanrio Co. Ltd.*

Japan Airlines® Bag. This is a
fantastic example of an early
promotional piece from Japan Air
Lines. During the '70s in Japan
there was a surge of interest in
travel and Kitty was right on top of
this trend. $30-35, 1976.

Red Coin Purse. $5-10, 1994.

Red Patent Purse.
$10, 1999.

Drawstring Beach Bag. $10, 1999.

55

25th Anniversary Drawstring Bag. $15-20, 1999.

Blue Tote. $5-10, 2000.

Brilliant Green Tote. $5-10, 2001.

Sequined Purse. $15, 2001. *Courtesy of Sanrio Co. Ltd.*

Mini Polka Dot Satchel. $15-20, 2001.

Chic KT Logo Bag.
$15-20, 2002.

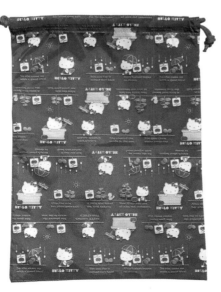

Plush Kitty Wristlet. $5, 2004.

Lux Wallet. $20, 2004.

Lavender Polka Dot Clutch. $15, 2004.
Courtesy of HighIntencity® Corp.

Kitty Face Bag. $15, 2004.

Drawstring Retro Shopper. This design was
originally used on a handkerchief in 1976.
$10, 2004.

Suede Wallet. $15, 2004. *Courtesy of Sanrio Co. Ltd.*

Suede Checkbook Cover. $15, 2004. *Courtesy of Sanrio Co. Ltd.*

Carry-All from *The Strawberry News*. $10, 2004.

Suede Shoulder Bag. $20, 2004. *Courtesy of Sanrio Co. Ltd.*

First Cell Phone. $30-35, 1994.
Courtesy of Sanrio Co. Ltd.

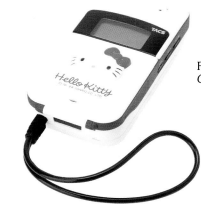

Reproduction Coin Purse from *The Strawberry News.* $20, 2004.

Call Me Kitty

Hello Kitty Model A3014S Cell Phone. Only released in Japan. $400, 2002. *Courtesy of Sony Ericsson Mobile Communications*

Pink Cell Phone Case. A huge hit in 1997 was the introduction of the pink pearl quilted series. $20, 1997. *Courtesy of Sanrio Co. Ltd.*

Chapter Twelve

You Can Never Have Too Many Friends

Kitty Quotes ~ "If You're Looking For The Purrfect Pal...She's The Cat's Meow" 1989

Dear Julius,

Hello! My name is Kitty. Perhaps you have already heard from Paul Frank that he ran into my friend Yuko Yamaguchi while she was visiting San Francisco? Good news, we are going to work together!

I am very excited as this is one of my first collaborations. My New Year's wish for 2002 was to make more friends and now it is coming true.

Do you have any hobbies, Julius? I play tennis. If you play, bring your racket. There is a court near my home.

See you soon.

Hugs, Kitty ✿

Cosmetic Bag In Light Blue. Kitty shares her passion for tennis with Julius. *Courtesy of Paul Frank Industries Inc.*

Kitty Tales ~ Paul Frank's Hello Kitty collection sold out only a few days after it was released in Spring 2002.

Hand Bag In Yellow. With a little help from their friends, the duo sets out to build a doghouse. 2002. *Courtesy of Paul Frank Industries Inc.*

Coin purse In Yellow. 2002. *Courtesy of Paul Frank Industries Inc.*

Shoulder Bag In Lilac. Julius and Kitty on a blue Vespa check out the city. Only 350 of this limited edition bag were produced. 2002. *Courtesy of Paul Frank Industries Inc.*

CD Case In Blue. The newest figure skating pairs couple, Julius & Kitty. Looks like a gold medal! 2002. *Courtesy of Paul Frank Industries Inc.*

Chapter Thirteen

The Cat's Meow ✿

Kitty Quotes ~ "Greet The Sun With A Big Hello" 1978

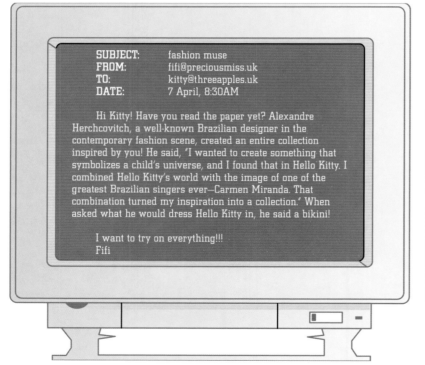

SUBJECT: fashion muse
FROM: fifi@preciousmiss.uk
TO: kitty@threeapples.uk
DATE: 7 April, 8:30AM

Hi Kitty! Have you read the paper yet? Alexandre Herchcovitch, a well-known Brazilian designer in the contemporary fashion scene, created an entire collection inspired by you! He said, 'I wanted to create something that symbolizes a child's universe, and I found that in Hello Kitty. I combined Hello Kitty's world with the image of one of the greatest Brazilian singers ever—Carmen Miranda. That combination turned my inspiration into a collection." When asked what he would dress Hello Kitty in, he said a bikini!

I want to try on everything!!!
Fifi

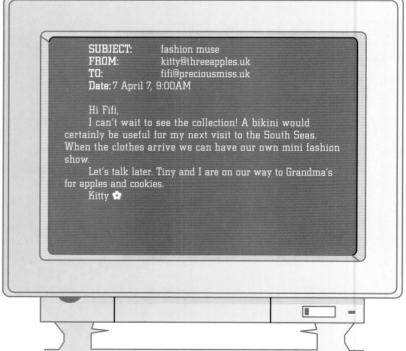

SUBJECT: fashion muse
FROM: kitty@threeapples.uk
TO: fifi@preciousmiss.uk
Date: 7 April 7, 9:00AM

Hi Fifi,
I can't wait to see the collection! A bikini would certainly be useful for my next visit to the South Seas. When the clothes arrive we can have our own mini fashion show.
Let's talk later. Tiny and I are on our way to Grandma's for apples and cookies.
Kitty ✿

Autumn/Winter 2004 Collection. A Hello Kitty face is printed on georgette silk, viscose, and cotton jersey. *Courtesy of Alexandre Herchcovitch / People's Revolution*

Autumn/Winter 2004 Collection. *Courtesy of Alexandre Herchcovitch / People's Revolution*

 Go In Style

Kitty Compact. $10-15, 1989.

Kitty & Cathy Brooch. $5-10, 1998.

Bracelet. $5-8, 1998.

Rhinestone Ring. $5, 2004. *Courtesy of Sanrio Co. Ltd.*

Rhinestone Compact Mirror. $35, 2004. *Courtesy of Sanrio Co. Ltd.*

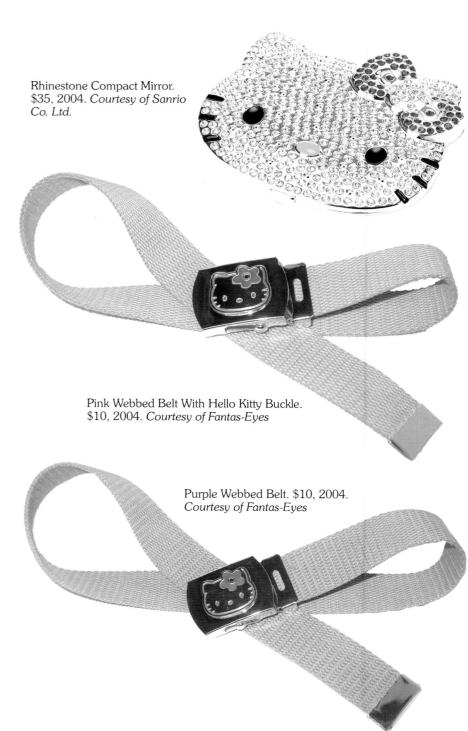

Rhinestone Hairclip Set. $2, 2004. *Courtesy of Sanrio Co. Ltd.*

Pink Webbed Belt With Hello Kitty Buckle. $10, 2004. *Courtesy of Fantas-Eyes*

Purple Webbed Belt. $10, 2004. *Courtesy of Fantas-Eyes*

Rhinestone Belt Buckle. $20, 2004. *Courtesy of Sanrio Co. Ltd.*

Pink Bracelet. Large faceted beads with satin bow and Hello Kitty charm. $5, 2004. *Courtesy of Fantas-Eyes*

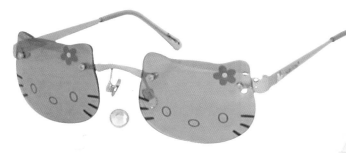

Pink Rimless Sunglasses. $5, 2004. *Courtesy of Fantas-Eyes*

Double Chain Necklace. Pink faceted beaded drops and Hello Kitty rhinestone heart pendent. $5, 2004. *Courtesy of Fantas-Eyes*

Rimless Sunglasses. Details include rhinestones on top of the lens and a tiny Hello Kitty image in the corner. $5, 2004. *Courtesy of Fantas-Eyes*

Chapter Fourteen

Charmed To Meet You ❀

Kitty Quotes ~ "I'm The Happiest Little Girl In The Whole World" 1990

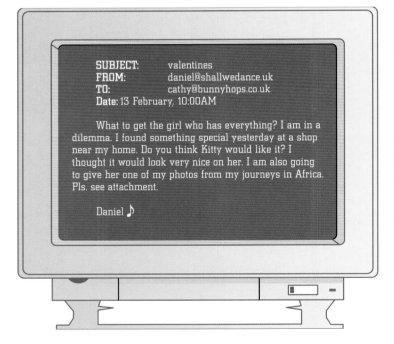

SUBJECT: valentines
FROM: daniel@shallwedance.uk
TO: cathy@bunnyhops.co.uk
Date: 13 February, 10:00AM

What to get the girl who has everything? I am in a dilemma. I found something special yesterday at a shop near my home. Do you think Kitty would like it? I thought it would look very nice on her. I am also going to give her one of my photos from my journeys in Africa. Pls. see attachment.

Daniel ♪

SUBJECT: valentines
FROM: cathy@bunnyhops.co.uk
TO: daniel@shallwedance.uk
DATE: 13 February, 10:30AM

Dear Daniel, How lovely! I am sure she will be quite pleased. You should definitely include one of your photos as well. I have to finish my Valentines for school. "If you're looking for the purrfect pal...She's the cat's meow." Guess Who?!

See you tomorrow.
Cathy

Glitter Enamel Jean Clip. 2004.
Courtesy of HighItencity® Corp.

Enamel Link Pin. 2004.
Courtesy of HighItencity® Corp.

Enamel Charms &
Bracelet. 2004. *Courtesy
of HighItencity® Corp.*

Charm Poster. 2003. *Courtesy of Casa D'Oro®*

Column one, top to bottom:

Red Bow. $15, 2003. *Courtesy of Casa D'Oro®*

Flower. $15, 2003. *Courtesy of Casa D'Oro®*

Convertible. $15, 2003. *Courtesy of Casa D'Oro®*

Chef. $20, 2003. *Courtesy of Casa D'Oro®*

Princess. $20, 2003. *Courtesy of Casa D'Oro®*

Shopping. $20, 2003. *Courtesy of Casa D'Oro®*

Kimono. $20, 2003. *Courtesy of Casa D'Oro®*

Column two, top to bottom:

Purple Butterfly Kitty. $20, 2003. *Courtesy of Casa D'Oro®*

Peek-A-Boo. $20, 2003. *Courtesy of Casa D'Oro®*

Dolphin. $20, 2003. *Courtesy of Casa D'Oro®*

Waving Kitty. $20, 2003. *Courtesy of Casa D'Oro®*

Bouquet. $20, 2003. *Courtesy of Casa D'Oro®*

Hands Up. $20, 2003. *Courtesy of Casa D'Oro®*

Guitar. $20, 2003. *Courtesy of Casa D'Oro®*

Holiday Kitty

Column one, top to bottom:

Statue Of Liberty. $20, 2003. *Courtesy of Casa D'Oro®*

Easter Bunny. $20, 2003. *Courtesy of Casa D'Oro®*

Love Kitty. $20, 2003. *Courtesy of Casa D'Oro®*

Love You Kitty. $20, 2003. *Courtesy of Casa D'Oro®*

Peek-A-Boo Heart. $20, 2003. *Courtesy of Casa D'Oro®*

Large Red Heart. $20, 2003. *Courtesy of Casa D'Oro®*

Column two, top to bottom:

Dangling Heart. $20, 2003. *Courtesy of Casa D'Oro®*

Candy Cane. $20, 2003. *Courtesy of Casa D'Oro®*

Santa Cap. $20, 2003. *Courtesy of Casa D'Oro®*

Devil. $20, 2003. *Courtesy of Casa D'Oro®*

Angel Kitty

Far left:
Pink Angel. $20, 2003. *Courtesy of Casa D'Oro®*

Left:
Blue Angel. $20, 2003. *Courtesy of Casa D'Oro®*

Sporty Kitty

Column one, top to bottom:

Ballerina. $20, 2003. *Courtesy of Casa D'Oro®*

Cheerleader. $20, 2003. *Courtesy of Casa D'Oro®*

Cyclist. $20, 2003. *Courtesy of Casa D'Oro®*

Surfer. $20, 2003. *Courtesy of Casa D'Oro®*

Ice Skater. $20, 2003. *Courtesy of Casa D'Oro®*

Column two, top to bottom:

Swimmer. $20, 2003. *Courtesy of Casa D'Oro®*

Tennis Player. $20, 2003. *Courtesy of Casa D'Oro®*

Soccer Player. $20, 2003. *Courtesy of Casa D'Oro®*

Rodeo Gal. $20, 2003. *Courtesy of Casa D'Oro®*

Rodeo Gal With Lasso. $20, 2003. *Courtesy of Casa D'Oro®*

Kitty 's Friends

Column one, top to bottom:

Tiny Chum Angel. $15, 2003. *Courtesy of Casa D'Oro®*

Rory. $15, 2003. *Courtesy of Casa D'Oro®*

Joey. $15, 2003. *Courtesy of Casa D'Oro®*

Column two, top to bottom:

Tammy. $15, 2003. *Courtesy of Casa D'Oro®*

Tim. $15, 2003. *Courtesy of Casa D'Oro®*

Penguin. $15, 2003. *Courtesy of Casa D'Oro®*

Tea Time Kitty

Column one, top to bottom:

Teapot. $15, 2003. *Courtesy of Casa D'Oro®*

Teacup. $15, 2003. *Courtesy of Casa D'Oro®*

Popsicle. $15, 2003. *Courtesy of Casa D'Oro®*

Column two, top to bottom:

Cupcake. $15, 2003. *Courtesy of Casa D'Oro®*

Strawberry Shortcake. $15, 2003. *Courtesy of Casa D'Oro®*

Ice Cream Cone. $15, 2003. *Courtesy of Casa D'Oro®*

Kitty Quotes ~ "Time Passes Most of Us In Ways Hard
To See & What We Do Is Soon Memories" 1987

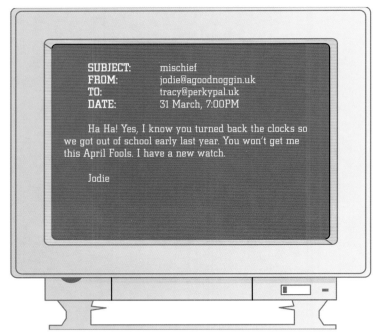

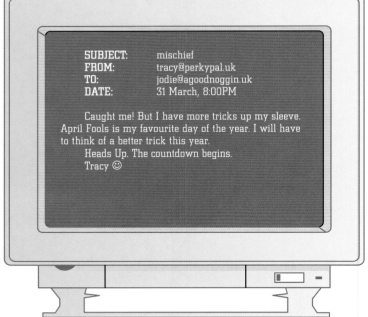

SUBJECT: mischief
FROM: jodie@agoodnoggin.uk
TO: tracy@perkypal.uk
DATE: 31 March, 7:00PM

Ha Ha! Yes, I know you turned back the clocks so we got out of school early last year. You won't get me this April Fools. I have a new watch.

Jodie

SUBJECT: mischief
FROM: tracy@perkypal.uk
TO: jodie@agoodnoggin.uk
DATE: 31 March, 8:00PM

Caught me! But I have more tricks up my sleeve. April Fools is my favourite day of the year. I will have to think of a better trick this year.
Heads Up. The countdown begins.
Tracy ☺

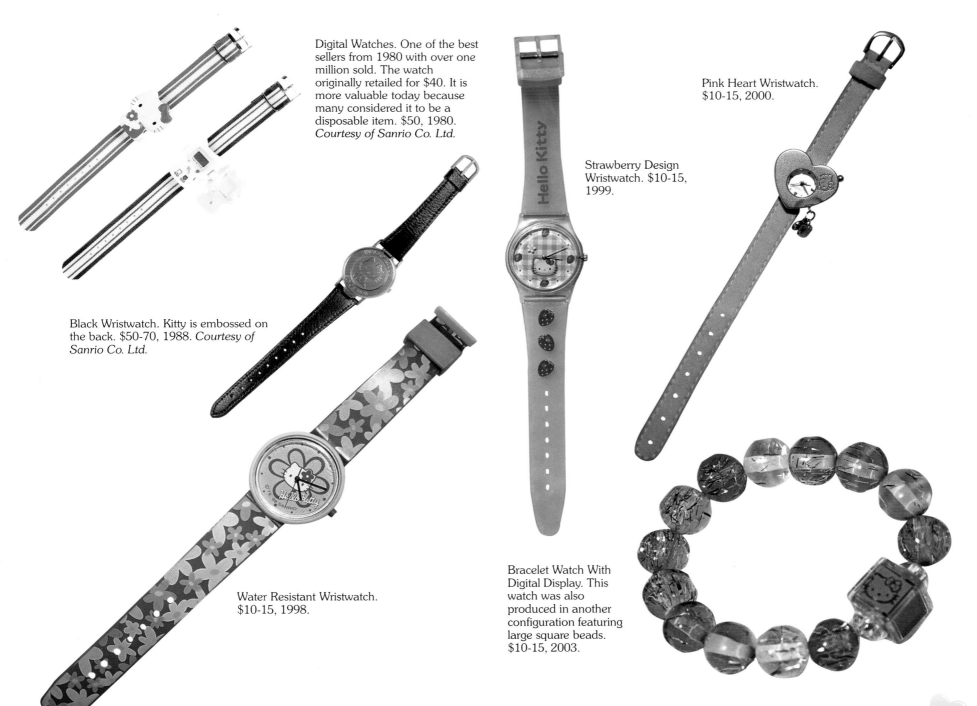

Digital Watches. One of the best sellers from 1980 with over one million sold. The watch originally retailed for $40. It is more valuable today because many considered it to be a disposable item. $50, 1980. *Courtesy of Sanrio Co. Ltd.*

Strawberry Design Wristwatch. $10-15, 1999.

Pink Heart Wristwatch. $10-15, 2000.

Black Wristwatch. Kitty is embossed on the back. $50-70, 1988. *Courtesy of Sanrio Co. Ltd.*

Water Resistant Wristwatch. $10-15, 1998.

Bracelet Watch With Digital Display. This watch was also produced in another configuration featuring large square beads. $10-15, 2003.

Snap On Charm Watch. Came with inter-changeable charms. $12, 2004. *Courtesy of Takara® USA Inc.*

Wristwatches. Red leather strap with metal eyelets and fancy buckle. White leather band with printed pattern and silver case. 2005. *Courtesy of MZ Berger & Company.*

Aqua Watches. See Kitty swim with a dolphin or play in her garden. $15, 2004. *Courtesy of Takara® USA Inc.*

Gold Metal Link Bracelet Watch and Wristwatch With Heart Shaped Stones. Metal case with art printed on sunray dial and applied logo. 2005. *Courtesy of MZ Berger & Company.*

Wall Clock. *Courtesy of MZ Berger & Company.*

Chapter Sixteen

Go Go Kitty! ❀

Kitty Quotes ~ "We Like To Ride Our Tricycles On Such Nice Days" 1977

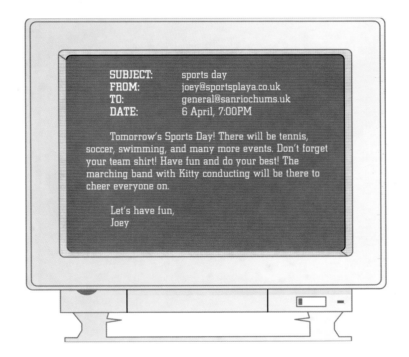

SUBJECT: sports day
FROM: joey@sportsplaya.co.uk
TO: general@sanriochums.uk
DATE: 6 April, 7:00PM

Tomorrow's Sports Day! There will be tennis, soccer, swimming, and many more events. Don't forget your team shirt! Have fun and do your best! The marching band with Kitty conducting will be there to cheer everyone on.

Let's have fun,
Joey

Surfer Kitty Single Speed Coaster Bike.
$300, 2004. *Courtesy of Nirve*®

Retro Kitty Cruiser. $240, 2004. *Courtesy of Nirve*®

Little Kitty 16" Pink Bike. $110, 2004. *Courtesy of Nirve®*

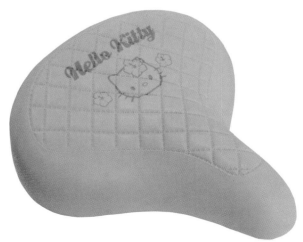

Pink Bike Seat. 2004. *Courtesy of Nirve®*

Kitty Tire Tread. 2004. *Courtesy of Nirve®*

White Bike Seat. 2004. *Courtesy of Nirve®*

Bowling 4 Kitty

 Beep, beep, beep! Here I Come!

Blue Viz-A-Ball. As of December 2004 only 1,000 balls had been produced. 2004. *Courtesy of Brunswick® Bowling & Billiards*

Vespa. Wow! The ultimate ride for the Hello Kitty fan. $2000, 1999. *Courtesy of Yamaha*

Pink Viz-A-Ball. $100, 2004. *Courtesy of Brunswick® Bowling & Billiards*

Lemon Car Air Freshener.
$1-3, 1998.

Camp Light With Handle.
Courtesy of Rayovac®

Lemon Car Air Freshener.
$1-3, 1998.

Mini Keychain Flashlight.
Courtesy of Rayovac®

Chapter Seventeen

From Kitty's Home To Yours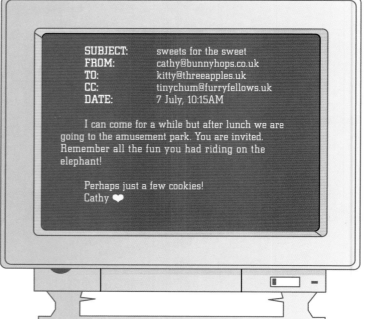

Kitty Quotes ~ "Good Health Starts With Cleanliness" 1996

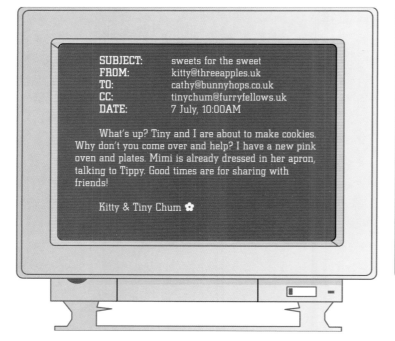

SUBJECT: sweets for the sweet
FROM: kitty@threeapples.uk
TO: cathy@bunnyhops.co.uk
CC: tinychum@furryfellows.uk
DATE: 7 July, 10:00AM

What's up? Tiny and I are about to make cookies. Why don't you come over and help? I have a new pink oven and plates. Mimi is already dressed in her apron, talking to Tippy. Good times are for sharing with friends!

Kitty & Tiny Chum ✿

SUBJECT: sweets for the sweet
FROM: cathy@bunnyhops.co.uk
TO: kitty@threeapples.uk
CC: tinychum@furryfellows.uk
DATE: 7 July, 10:15AM

I can come for a while but after lunch we are going to the amusement park. You are invited. Remember all the fun you had riding on the elephant!

Perhaps just a few cookies!
Cathy ♥

Child's Chopsticks.
$1, 1994.

Slim Thermos &
Cover. $5-10,
1998.

Spoon. $1, 2000.

Dish Set.
$2, 2001.

Red Snack Container. $1, 1998.

Snack Containers.
$3-5, 2001

PEZ® Dispensers. One of the most anticipated releases in 2003 was the Hello Kitty PEZ. $20-25, 2003. *Courtesy of PEZ Candy, Inc.*

In The Kitchen With Kitty

Pink Container.
$5, 2001

Hello Kitty Snow Cone Maker. $20, 2000. *Courtesy of Blue Box Toys*

Utensil Set. $5, 2003

Kitty Tales ~ A huge assortment of Kitty candy, gum, chocolate, snacks and even instant noodles are sold in Japan. Yum!

Pop Up Toaster. $40, 2004. *Courtesy of Sanyo™ Home Appliances*

Milk Shake Maker. $30, 2004. *Courtesy of Spectra® Merchandising International*

Mini Water Dispenser. $16, 2004. *Courtesy of Spectra® Merchandising International*

Waffle Maker. $40, 2004. *Courtesy of Spectra® Merchandising International*

Sandwich Maker. $40, 2004. *Courtesy of Sanyo™ Home Appliances*

Mini Refrigerator. $40, 2004. *Courtesy of Spectra® Merchandising International*

Kitchen Wear

Child's Apron.
$5-10, 2001.

Adult's Apron.
$10-15, 2001.

Japan Air Systems® Bib Holder. Came with interchangeable stickers featuring Hello Kitty and Daniel dressed as JAS stewards. $5-10, 2002.

Chapter Eighteen
Kitty Power ❀

Kitty Quotes ~ "This Is A Good Day 'Cause I'm With You"1991

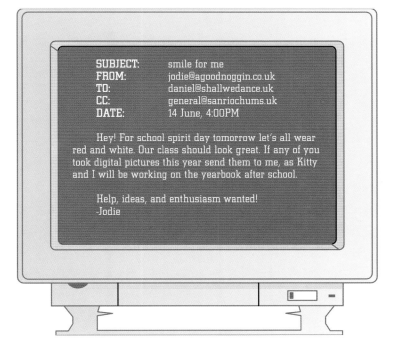

SUBJECT: smile for me
FROM: jodie@agoodnoggin.co.uk
TO: daniel@shallwedance.uk
CC: general@sanriochums.uk
DATE: 14 June, 4:00PM

Hey! For school spirit day tomorrow let's all wear red and white. Our class should look great. If any of you took digital pictures this year send them to me, as Kitty and I will be working on the yearbook after school.

Help, ideas, and enthusiasm wanted!
-Jodie

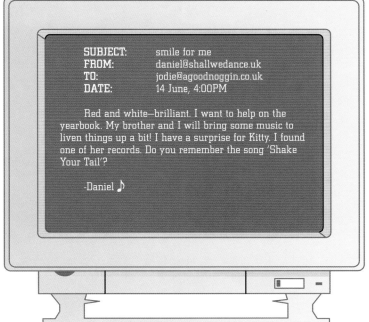

SUBJECT: smile for me
FROM: daniel@shallwedance.uk
TO: jodie@agoodnoggin.co.uk
DATE: 14 June, 4:00PM

Red and white—brilliant. I want to help on the yearbook. My brother and I will bring some music to liven things up a bit! I have a surprise for Kitty. I found one of her records. Do you remember the song 'Shake Your Tail'?

-Daniel ♪

Kitty Sing Along

Portable Karaoke System. $40, 2004. *Courtesy of Spectra® Merchandising International*

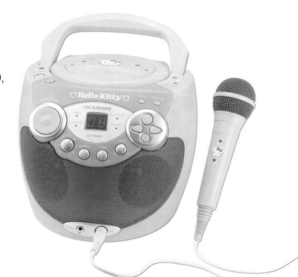

Stereo CD Boombox. $50, 2004. *Courtesy of Spectra® Merchandising International*

Personal CD Player. $40, 2004. *Courtesy of Spectra® Merchandising International*

Portable CD Player. $40, 2004. *Courtesy of Spectra® Merchandising International*

Handbag-Style Personal Cassette Player With Alarm Clock. $40, 2004. *Courtesy of Spectra® Merchandising International*

Pocketbook Stereo CD Player With Handles. $40, 2004. *Courtesy of Spectra® Merchandising International*

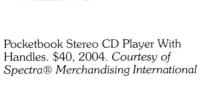

Rise & Shine Kitty

Standing Kitty Clock.
$20-25, 1992.

Ice Cream Clock Radio. $20,
2004. *Courtesy of Spectra®*
Merchandising International

Mini FM Radio With Earphones.
$20, 2001. *Courtesy of Spectra®*
Merchandising International

Digital Clock Radio.
Courtesy of Spectra®
Merchandising International

Shower Radio With Built In Clock.
$20, 2004. *Courtesy of Spectra®*
Merchandising International

 Kitty Vision

Suitcase Design 13" Color TV. $120, 2005. *Courtesy of Spectra® Merchandising International*

Sanrio's 30th Anniversary Kitty Television. Only 3,000 were ever produced. It originally retailed for $600. $1000, 1989. *Courtesy of Sanrio Co. Ltd.*

13" Stereo/Color TV/DVD Combo. $150, 2005. *Courtesy of Spectra® Merchandising International*

Remote Control 13" Color Television. $150, 2004. *Courtesy of Spectra® Merchandising International*

DVD Player With Remote Control. $110, 2005. *Courtesy of Spectra® Merchandising International*

Kitty Automatic Camera. The camera was also released in red. Both versions made quite a splash during their release year. $200-250, 1982. *Courtesy of Sanrio Co. Ltd.*

Fujicolor album. $1-3, 1997.

Digital Camera. $50, 2004. *Courtesy of Spectra Merchandising International*

Pink Photo Album. $1-3, 1997.

Chapter Nineteen

Dream A Little Dream 🌸

Kitty Quotes ~ "Hearts & Flowers Brighten My Day!" 1992

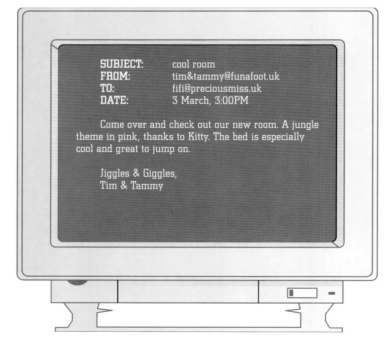

SUBJECT: cool room
FROM: tim&tammy@funafoot.uk
TO: fifi@preciousmiss.uk
DATE: 3 March, 3:00PM

Come over and check out our new room. A jungle theme in pink, thanks to Kitty. The bed is especially cool and great to jump on.

Jiggles & Giggles,
Tim & Tammy

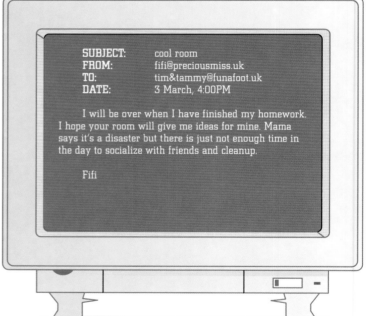

SUBJECT: cool room
FROM: fifi@preciousmiss.uk
TO: tim&tammy@funafoot.uk
DATE: 3 March, 4:00PM

I will be over when I have finished my homework. I hope your room will give me ideas for mine. Mama says it's a disaster but there is just not enough time in the day to socialize with friends and cleanup.

Fifi

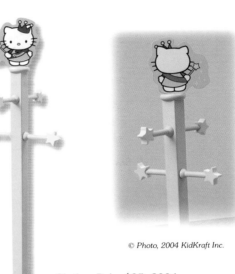

Table & Chair. $50, 2004. *Courtesy of KidKraft® Inc.*

Clothes Pole. $35, 2004. *Courtesy of KidKraft® Inc.*

TV Tray. $45, 2004. *Courtesy of KidKraft® Inc.*

Storage Stool. $20, 2004. *Courtesy of KidKraft® Inc.*

Wall Shelf. $40, 2004. *Courtesy of KidKraft® Inc.*

Keepsake Purse. $20, 2004.
Courtesy of KidKraft® Inc.

© *Photo, 2004 KidKraft Inc.*

Dress-Up Mirror. $75, 2004.
Courtesy of KidKraft® Inc.

© *Photo, 2004 KidKraft Inc.*

© *Photo, 2004 KidKraft Inc.*

Mini Vanity mirror. $25, 2004.
Courtesy of KidKraft® Inc.

© *Photo, 2004 KidKraft Inc.*

Hello Kitty
4 x 6 Photo Frame

KidKraft
Made in China
4630 Olin Road
Dallas, Tx 75224

Photo Frame

Sanrio
©1976, 2004 SANRIO CO., LTD.
Used Under License.
www.sanrio.com

Hello Kitty

Princess

Frame. $15, 2004. *Courtesy of KidKraft® Inc.*

© *Photo, 2004 KidKraft Inc.*

Handheld Mirror. $20, 2004.
Courtesy of KidKraft® Inc.

Keepsake Box. $20, 2004.
Courtesy of KidKraft® Inc.

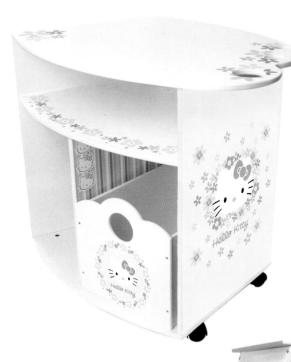

TV & Stereo Stand. $95,
2004. *Courtesy of
KidKraft® Inc.*

Mini Armoire. $20,
2004. *Courtesy of
KidKraft® Inc.*

Storage Cart With Drawers. $110,
2004. *Courtesy of KidKraft® Inc.*

Toddler
Bedding.
$65, 2004.
*Courtesy of
Lambs &
Ivy®*

Blanket. $20, 2004.
Courtesy of Lambs & Ivy®

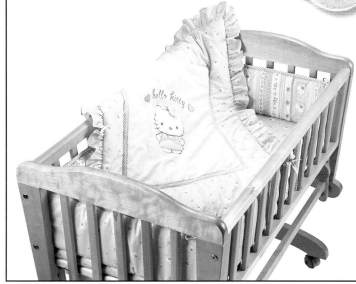

Cradle bedding.
$65, 2004.
*Courtesy of
Lambs & Ivy®*

Hamper. $30, 2004.
*Courtesy of Lambs &
Ivy®*

Shelf. $30, 2004. *Courtesy of Lambs & Ivy®*

Drawer Liner. $10, 2004.
Courtesy of Lambs & Ivy®

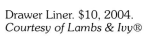

Drawer Pulls. $10, 2004.
Courtesy of Lambs & Ivy®

92

Lamp. $45, 2004.
Courtesy of Lambs & Ivy®

Rug. $35, 2004. *Courtesy of Lambs & Ivy®*

Summer Pajama Set. $20-25, 2002.

 Sweet Dreams Kitty

 Wash Your Mittens

Pink comb. $1, 2001.

Red slippers with bold faces of Kitty, Cathy, and Tiny Chum. $2-5, 2000.

French Angel trinket box. $5-10, 2001.

Bubble Bath. 2001.

Hand Towel. $2-5, 2002.

Nail Vanity. $10, 2004. *Courtesy of JAKKS Pacific, Inc.*

Kitty Tales ~ Kitty has really branched out into cosmetics and perfume in Japan with her own Hello Kitty Eau de Toilette.

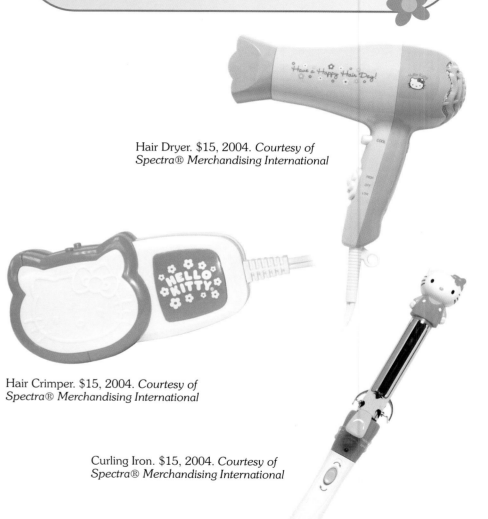

Hair Dryer. $15, 2004. *Courtesy of Spectra® Merchandising International*

Hair Crimper. $15, 2004. *Courtesy of Spectra® Merchandising International*

Curling Iron. $15, 2004. *Courtesy of Spectra® Merchandising International*

Chapter Twenty

Candles 4 Kitty ✿

Kitty Quotes ~ "When I'm With Friends I Feel So Wonderful" 1993

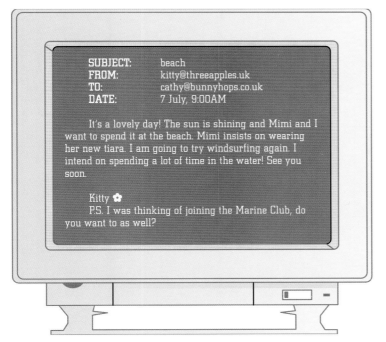

SUBJECT: beach
FROM: kitty@threeapples.uk
TO: cathy@bunnyhops.co.uk
DATE: 7 July, 9:00AM

It's a lovely day! The sun is shining and Mimi and I want to spend it at the beach. Mimi insists on wearing her new tiara. I am going to try windsurfing again. I intend on spending a lot of time in the water! See you soon.

Kitty ✿
P.S. I was thinking of joining the Marine Club, do you want to as well?

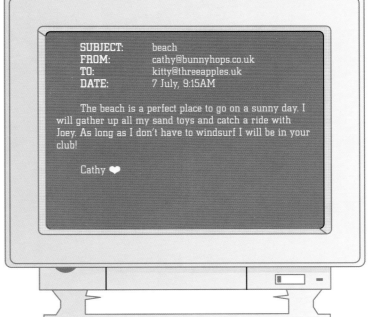

SUBJECT: beach
FROM: cathy@bunnyhops.co.uk
TO: kitty@threeapples.uk
DATE: 7 July, 9:15AM

The beach is a perfect place to go on a sunny day. I will gather up all my sand toys and catch a ride with Joey. As long as I don't have to windsurf I will be in your club!

Cathy ♥

Limited Edition NEC LaVie G Type J' Ultralight Laptop. Only 300 were produced by NEC to help celebrate Hello Kitty's 30th Anniversary. Approx. $2,500 retail, 2004. *Courtesy of NEC*

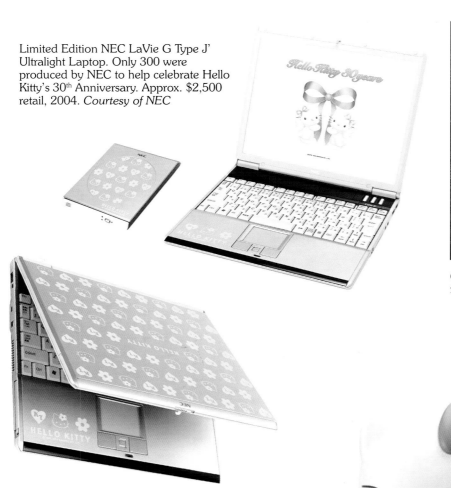

Coin Set. Six coins ranging in value from 1¥ to 500¥ and a special bonus Hello Kitty coin from the Japanese mint. $30-35, 2004. *Courtesy of Sanrio Co. Ltd.*

Hello Kitty Robo. 2004. *Courtesy of Courtesy of Business Design Laboratory Co., Ltd.*

Hello Kitty Robo. You can chat with Hello Kitty. She can talk on a variety of subjects. $4,330, 2004. *Courtesy of Business Design Laboratory Co., Ltd.*

Sanrio Vintage Mini. Twelve different sets, with thirty-eight items total, were made for sale in Japan only. $70-80 for all twelve, 2004.

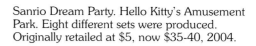

Sanrio Dream Party. Hello Kitty's Amusement Park. Eight different sets were produced. Originally retailed at $5, now $35-40, 2004.

Hello Kitty 30 Years Phone Card. $5, 2004.

30th Anniversary Collection Clock. Each shadow box contained a miniature replica of a popular item from each of Kitty's thirty years. $300, 2004. *Courtesy of Mayumi Kuribayashi*

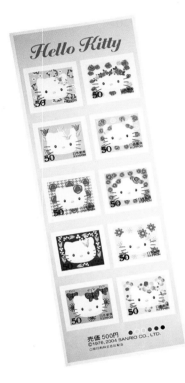

Hello Kitty 80 Yen
Stamp Set. $10, 2004.

White Clutch. $40, 2004.

Hello Kitty 50 Yen
Stamp Set. $5, 2004.

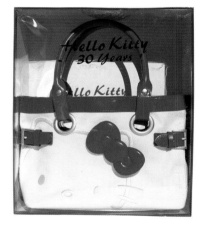

Small Tote With Signature Red Handles.
Shown in its original box. $60, 2004.
Courtesy of Kaylee Emi Yasuda

 Kitty Ribbon Limited Goods

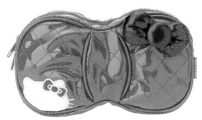

Quilted Ribbon Clutch. A
logo and check design were
also produced. $12, 2004.
Courtesy of Sanrio Co. Ltd.

Pink & White Ribbon T-Shirts. The white t-shirt came with an alternate pink bow to suit any mood. $30, 2004. *Courtesy of Sanrio Co. Ltd.*

Platinum Doll. The doll is 4.1 cm in height. Ball gown encrusted with diamonds. Only 30 were produced. Originally retailed for $28,000, later sold for $100,000 at auction, 2004. *Courtesy of Sanrio Co. Ltd.*

Diamond & Ruby Eternity Ring. $150, 2004.

Royal Tiara. Seventy-five cubic zirconium diamonds embellish the tiara, which came complete with it's own pink keepsake box. $800, 2004. *Courtesy of Sanrio Co. Ltd.*

Mirror With Kitty Check Design. $20, 2004. *Courtesy of Sanrio Co. Ltd.*

Lacquer Box With Gold Coin Kitty. Only 1,000 one ounce coins were produced and 2,000, one-quarter-once coins. Six different designs based on a heroine from a *kabuki* play were produced. *Courtesy of Sanrio Co. Ltd.*

Chapter Twenty-One

Kitty Has A Big Heart ✿

Kitty Quotes ~ "We're So Lucky To Have Each Other" 1988

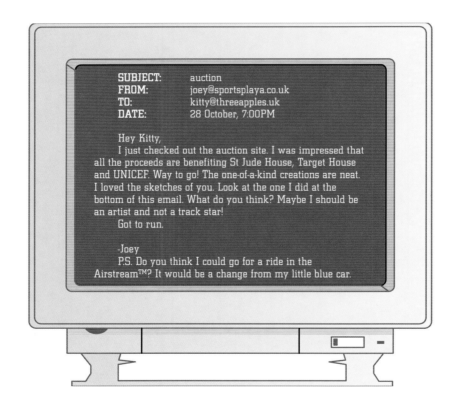

SUBJECT: auction
FROM: joey@sportsplaya.co.uk
TO: kitty@threeapples.uk
DATE: 28 October, 7:00PM

Hey Kitty,
     I just checked out the auction site. I was impressed that all the proceeds are benefiting St Jude House, Target House and UNICEF. Way to go! The one-of-a-kind creations are neat. I loved the sketches of you. Look at the one I did at the bottom of this email. What do you think? Maybe I should be an artist and not a track star!
     Got to run.

-Joey
     P.S. Do you think I could go for a ride in the Airstream™? It would be a change from my little blue car.

Kimora Lee Simmons Diamond Charm Bracelet. A, 18K white gold link chain, Hello Kitty shaped diamond-encrusted charms and a heart lock. $10,000, 2004. *Courtesy of Sanrio Co., Ltd.*

Steve Madden Hello Kitty Shoes. $500, 2004. *Courtesy of Sanrio Co., Ltd.*

Eugenia Kim Hello Kitty Beret. "I love the perfect-ness of Hello Kitty as a brand and icon, and wanted to make a HK hat that looked like a pill/cake!" said Eugenia Kim. $455, 2004. *Courtesy of Sanrio Co., Ltd.*

Steve Madden Hello Kitty Satin Stiletto Boots. Shiny gold studs accent Hello Kitty's image. $1025, 2004. *Courtesy of Sanrio Co., Ltd.*

Betsey Johnson Ruffled Corset Dress. The bodice is laced with a black velvet ribbon and the skirt is composed of tiers of ruffles. 2004. *Courtesy of Sanrio Co., Ltd.*

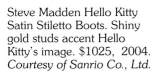

101

BCBG Max Azria® Hello Kitty Silk & Cashmere Cardiwrap Sweater. On the back of this garment is a Hello Kitty face studded with Swarovski® crystals. $5000, 2004. *Courtesy of Sanrio Co., Ltd.*

Tiffany Dubin. 2004. *Courtesy of Sanrio Co., Ltd.*

Tiffany Dubin. 2004. *Courtesy of Sanrio Co., Ltd.*

Esteban Cortazar Organza Mini Dress. A baby doll dress with Swarovski® crystals. $600, 2004. *Courtesy of Sanrio Co., Ltd.*

Sheri Bodell Halter-Top Jumpsuit. $355, 2004. *Courtesy of Sanrio Co., Ltd.*

Heatherette White Fringed Chaps. 2004. *Courtesy of Sanrio Co., Ltd.*

Heatherette White Kitty Tank. 2004.
Courtesy of Sanrio Co., Ltd.

Michael Graves Hello Kitty
Purrvilion. $1000, 2004.
Courtesy of Sanrio Co., Ltd.

Mossimo® Giannulli & Ernie
Ball® Hello Kitty Electric
Guitar. $2025, 2004. *Courtesy
of Sanrio Co., Ltd.*

Richard Walker Sun-
glasses. $500, 2004.
*Courtesy of Sanrio Co.,
Ltd.*

Richard Walker Sunglasses.
$500, 2004. *Courtesy of
Sanrio Co., Ltd.*

NYC Peach Sidekick™ II. 2004.
Courtesy of Sanrio Co., Ltd.

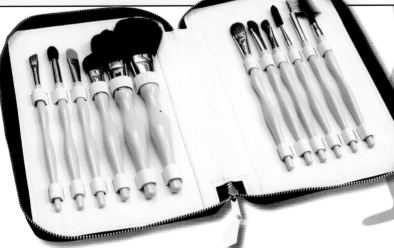

Sonia Kashuk Pink Brush Set. 2004. *Courtesy of Sanrio Co., Ltd.*

Nirve® 24K Gold Plated Kruiser. Custom airbrush painting, rhinestones on each Hello Kitty face, and twenty-four karat plating throughout. $6500, 2004. *Courtesy of Sanrio Co., Ltd.*

Tarina Tarantino Pink Chandelier. The chandelier came with a tag autographed by the designer, reading, *"Have a sparkling day!"* in pink. $3420, 2004. *Courtesy of Sanrio Co., Ltd.*

Rocky McKinnon Long Board. 2004. *Courtesy of Sanrio Co., Ltd.*

Sanrio Hello Kitty 25' Airstream™ Trailer International CCD. A huge Hello Kitty face and her name adorn the outside of this super-sweet Airstream™ Trailer. $50,100, 2004. *Courtesy of Sanrio Co., Ltd.*

Chapter Twenty-Two

Extra! Extra! Kitty Ex. ✿

Kitty Quotes ~ "When It Rains I'm Never Alone Under My Umbrella" 1988

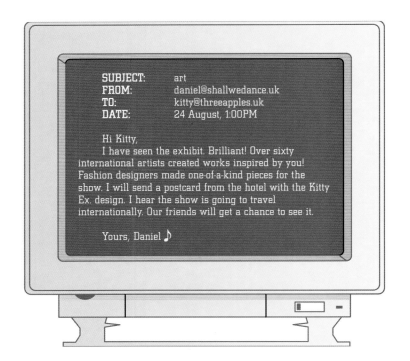

SUBJECT: art
FROM: daniel@shallwedance.uk
TO: kitty@threeapples.uk
DATE: 24 August, 1:00PM

Hi Kitty,
I have seen the exhibit. Brilliant! Over sixty international artists created works inspired by you! Fashion designers made one-of-a-kind pieces for the show. I will send a postcard from the hotel with the Kitty Ex. design. I hear the show is going to travel internationally. Our friends will get a chance to see it.

Yours, Daniel ♪

Lil'limo Handbag. A combination of textures including yarn, tapestry, and a pink rhinestone Kitty were used. 2004. *Courtesy of Digital Hollywood Entertainment Corp.*

Samantha Thavasa New York White Quilted Leather Bag. A luxurious line for the now grown-up Kitty. 2004. *Courtesy of Digital Hollywood Entertainment Corp.*

Lil'limo Shoes. 2004. *Courtesy of Digital Hollywood Entertainment Corp.*

Samantha Thavasa New York Red Patent Tote. 2004. *Courtesy of Digital Hollywood Entertainment Corp.*

A Mon Avis Stylish Black Handbag. The white trim was inspired by Kitty's fur. 2004. *Courtesy of Digital Hollywood Entertainment Corp.*

Samantha Thavasa New York Glamorous Gold Tote. 2004. *Courtesy of Digital Hollywood Entertainment Corp.*

Samantha Thavasa New York Bag. A modern silver bag just perfect for an evening out. 2004. *Courtesy of Digital Hollywood Entertainment Corp.*

Samantha Thavasa New York Gold Clutch. Jewel encrusted Kitty detail. 2004. *Courtesy of Digital Hollywood Entertainment Corp.*

Head Porter Sporty Bag. 2004. *Courtesy of Digital Hollywood Entertainment Corp.*

Honey Salon White & Pink Shoes. Accented with the words *So Cool* and an image of Kitty spinning records. 2004. *Courtesy of Digital Hollywood Entertainment Corp.*

Garcia Marquez Tote Bag. 2004. *Courtesy of Digital Hollywood Entertainment Corp.*

Honey Salon Pink & White Satin Clutches. 2004. *Courtesy of Digital Hollywood Entertainment Corp.*

Honey Salon Key Chain. 2004. *Courtesy of Digital Hollywood Entertainment Corp.*

Garcia Marquez Pouch. 2004. *Courtesy of Digital Hollywood Entertainment Corp.*

H.A.K. Fabric. Kitty in her classic seated pose on a dark rose embossed fabric. 2004. *Courtesy of Digital Hollywood Entertainment Corp.*

CA4LA Hat. The designers were inspired by childhood memories of Kitty stickers and their favorite stuffed Hello Kitty. 2004. *Courtesy of Digital Hollywood Entertainment Corp.*

Bottom center:
CA4LA Hat. 2004. *Courtesy of Digital Hollywood Entertainment Corp.*

Below:
Hackford & Song Bracelet. 2004. *Courtesy of Digital Hollywood Entertainment Corp.*

H.A.K. Fabric. Camouflage inspired fabric. 2004. *Courtesy of Digital Hollywood Entertainment Corp.*

Below:
Hanway Umbrellas. 2004. *Courtesy of Digital Hollywood Entertainment Corp.*

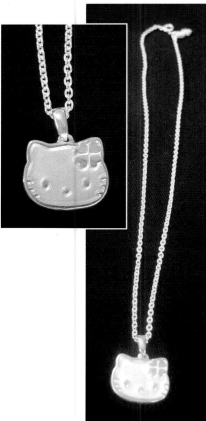

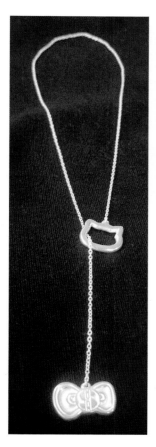

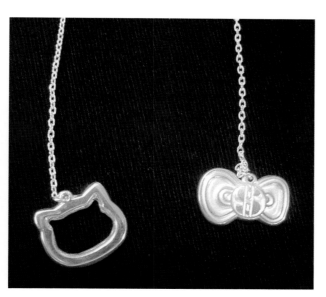

Hackford & Song Lariat. 2004. *Courtesy of Digital Hollywood Entertainment Corp.*

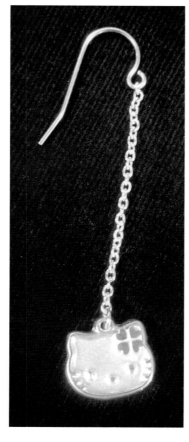

Hackford & Song Drop Earring. 2004. *Courtesy of Digital Hollywood Entertainment Corp.*

Loree Rodkin Necklace. 2004. *Courtesy of Digital Hollywood Entertainment Corp.*

Loree Rodkin. 2004. *Courtesy of Digital Hollywood Entertainment Corp.*

Loree Rodkin Ring. 2004. *Courtesy of Digital Hollywood Entertainment Corp.*

113

RUTA78 Drop Earrings. 2004. *Courtesy of Digital Hollywood Entertainment Corp.*

Left: White Trash Charms JAPAN Drop Earring. Letters K & T. 2004. *Courtesy of Digital Hollywood Entertainment Corp.*

Right: White Trash Charms JAPAN Drop Earring. Heart and Kitty. 2004. *Courtesy of Digital Hollywood Entertainment Corp.*

White Trash Charms JAPAN Necklace. Cubic zirconium accent Kitty 's bow. 2004. *Courtesy of Digital Hollywood Entertainment Corp.*

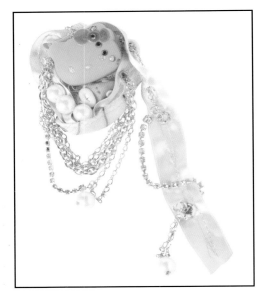

RUTA78 Brooch. 2004. *Courtesy of Digital Hollywood Entertainment Corp.*

RUTA78 Ring. 2004. *Courtesy of Digital Hollywood Entertainment Corp.*

White Trash Charms JAPAN I Luv Kitty Charm Bracelet. 2004. *Courtesy of Digital Hollywood Entertainment Corp.*

Tea For Two Gold Charm Bracelet. 2004. *Courtesy of Digital Hollywood Entertainment Corp.*

RUTA78 Brooch. 2004. *Courtesy of Digital Hollywood Entertainment Corp.*

White Trash Charms JAPAN Clip. 2004. *Courtesy of Digital Hollywood Entertainment Corp.*

Tea for Two Silver Charm Bracelet. 2004. *Courtesy of Digital Hollywood Entertainment Corp.*

Chapter Twenty-Three

We Love You. Who? You! ❀

*Kitty Quotes ~ "Friends Are The Most Important Ingredient In
Making Your Dreams Come True" 1995*

SUBJECT: give me an h-a-p-p-y
FROM: cathy@bunnyhops.co.uk
TO: kitty@threeapples.uk
DATE: 01 November, 8:00AM

Happy Birthday! You haven't changed a speck...well perhaps hair ribbons, but you're still the best! I hope we get to eat lots of ice cream. See you later on today.

Hugsies, Cathy 🖤

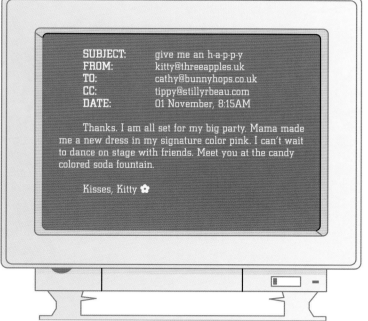

SUBJECT: give me an h-a-p-p-y
FROM: kitty@threeapples.uk
TO: cathy@bunnyhops.co.uk
CC: tippy@stillyrbeau.com
DATE: 01 November, 8:15AM

Thanks. I am all set for my big party. Mama made me a new dress in my signature color pink. I can't wait to dance on stage with friends. Meet you at the candy colored soda fountain.

Kisses, Kitty ✿

Celebrate Kitty USA

Hello Kitty at Rockefeller Center ~ On June 8th, 2004 the Hello Kitty 30th Anniversary season was officially launched by Sanrio in New York City. The UNICEF title 'Special Friend of Children', was given to Hello Kitty. Sanrio committed to donate a minimum of $150,000 to the US UNICEF for girls' education programs.

Hello Kitty Day at Shea Stadium ~ On August 15th 2004 Hello Kitty greeted and posed with fans prior to a baseball game between the NY METS and the Arizona Diamondbacks. Kitty threw out the first pitch. **Way to go Kitty!** The first 20,000 people were the lucky recipients of a free Hello Kitty doll dressed in a Mets uniform. Major League Baseball Hello Kitty dolls were introduced in Japan to celebrate the start of the 2004 baseball season. They are currently not available outside of Japan.

Hello Kitty Boardfest ~ Held at the Huntington Beach Pier in Orange County, California. In 2004 the event ran for three days, October 15-17. This was the second time Boardfest was ever held. It included a surf clinic, games, face painting, rock-climbing wall, sand castle building, a mechanical surfboard, and surfing, of course. The Hello Kitty Airstream™ trailer, which was later auctioned off for charity, also made an appearance. Boardfest also raised funds for UNICEF's School-in-a-Box initiative. The official website of the Hello Kitty Boardfest is <http://www.boardfest.com/>.

Hello Kitty Target UNICEF Charity Auction ~ This marked the third time that UNICEF and Hello Kitty have worked together. Proceeds from the auction went to charities that focused on children, Target House and UNICEF. Families whose children are undergoing lifesaving treatment at St. Jude live at Target House free of charge. For more information on these organizations please see the following web pages:

An enormous fuchsia cake was wheeled out onto the stage for Kitty's 30th birthday. *Courtesy of Sanrio Co. Ltd.*

UNICEF USA http://www.unicefusa.org

Target House
http://target.com/target_group/community_giving/target_house.jhtml

St. Jude Children's Research Hospital http://www.stjude.org

Hello Kitty 30th Anniversary Gala ~ The Raleigh Studios in Hollywood was transformed into a pink wonderland. Hello Kitty greeted her friends on the pink carpet. **All the best, Kitty!**

Celebrate Kitty Japan

Traveling Art Exhibit ~ Over 100 Japanese and international artists, designers, and musicians contributed Hello Kitty works to the show. Presented by Digital Hollywood Entertainment, the exhibit was first shown at Tokyo's Mori Museum and LaForet Museum from July 31st until August 29th, 2004. The exhibit included visual works, print art, tattoos, designer goods, and even an example of a Hello Kitty crop circle created by Surface To Air, a New York art group.

A mirror exhibition with a behind-the-scenes look at the Hello Kitty exhibit ran simultaneously. It was held at Tsutaya Tokyo Roppongi, a Japanese department store. This exhibit highlighted the construction process and prototypes for the items shown in the Mori Art Museum Kitty Ex. Show.

Hello Kitty Birthday Party ~ On November 1st, 2004, a huge 30th birthday party was held for Hello Kitty at the Sanrio Puroland theme park. Many people including Japanese celebrities, Yuko Yamaguchi, chief Hello Kitty designer, and Kitty herself attended the party.

Anniversary Exhibition Entrance. *Courtesy of Digital Hollywood Entertainment*

Left & bottom left:
Inside The Exhibition.
*Courtesy of Digital
Hollywood Entertainment*

Bottom center:
Anniversary Exhibition
Merchandise. *Courtesy of
Digital Hollywood Enter-
tainment*

Bottom right:
Tokyo City Bus With Kitty
Ex. Advertisement.
*Courtesy of Digital
Hollywood Entertainment*

Chapter Twenty-Four

There's No Place Like Home

Kitty Quotes ~ "There's A Spot In My Heart For Your Smile" 1998

Puroland

A giant shimmering rainbow marks the entrance to Puroland. Located in Tama-city Japan, it is one of the few fully enclosed theme parks in the world. There are three cheerful floors of fun activities, Sanrio characters, and Hello Kitty, of course.

After a short escalator ride, you arrive on the third floor of the park. A character, possibly Kitty, will be there to greet you. Pose for your own photo. **Click!**

Courtesy of Sanrio Co., Ltd.

Puroland boasts seven attractions, three restaurants, and the largest Sanrio store in the world! The daily parades and live shows will ensure that you stay entertained.

Access
Take the Odakyu-Tama Line or Hashimoto-bound Keio-Sagamihara Line to Tama Center Sta. It takes about thirty-five minutes by express train from Shinjuku.

Courtesy of Sanrio Co., Ltd.

Kitty's Tip ~ The local train has to stop at every station so be sure to get on the express. From Tama Center Station it will take 5-10 minutes to walk to the entrance gates.

Admission
Adult ¥4,400, Youth ¥4,000, and Child ¥3,300. A park passport will give you access to all events. There are lower evening rates so check out the site for full details. *Kitty's Tip* ~ For parents with small children, strollers are not permitted in Puroland so you will definitely need an infant carrier and a pair of strong shoulders!

Courtesy of Sanrio Co., Ltd.

Location
1-31 Ochiai, Tama-shi, Tokyo
Tel: 042-339-1111
The official Puroland Japanese website:
http://www.puroland.co.jp/
The official Puroland site in English:
http://www.sanrio.co.jp/english/spl/spl.html

Hours Of Operation
The park opens daily from 10AM to 5PM weekdays, until 8PM on Sundays and holidays. It is best to check with the main website as hours of operation may change. Closed the 2nd & 3rd Wednesdays and Thursdays of every month.

Services
Services include an information counter on the 1st and 3rd floors. There is a well-equipped baby center with change tables, lockers and even a place to courier

all your purchases back home. *__Kitty's Tip__* ~ The lockers located on the 3rd floor range in price from ¥100 to ¥400 so don't forget your ¥100 coins.

    Birthday Parties ~ If it is your special day, the park will be more than happy to celebrate it with you. Special drink holders, birthday hats, a Hello Kitty cake and menu are all available. Finish off your party by getting a picture taken with Kitty. *__Kitty's Tip__* ~ Ask in advance either online or by phone how to receive your special birthday present.

Courtesy of Sanrio Co., Ltd.

Attractions

Hello Kitty Musicals ~ There are always several live shows to go and see.

Kitty's Home ~ Kitty's home officially opened on October 23, 2004 after being remodelled in the Victorian style for her 30th birthday. From the shingles to the beautiful stained glass windows, it will leave all wishing that they lived in a pink home. The *Kittymobile* parked out front will leave you awestruck. **Vroooooom!**

Photo Mini Plant ~ With the aid of props, white paws, a bow and apron, you can become Kitty. **Say Cheese!**

Sanrio Character Boat Ride ~ A six-person boat ride will take you on a magical adventure through the world of Sanrio characters. Along the 300 meter canal you will pass by enchanted forests, treasure seekers, a space room, and a world of inventions—all accompanied by fairy-tale music. *__Kitty's Tip__* ~ Be sure to smile, as a commemorative photo will be available of your cruise through Puroland at Photo Mini Plant.

Starlight Parade of Characters ~ The lights are dimmed and a parade of costumed characters dance around the Tree of Wisdom. *__Kitty's Tip__* ~ Arrive at least thirty minutes early in order to get a seat.

Courtesy of Sanrio Co., Ltd.

Courtesy of Sanrio Co., Ltd.

Courtesy of Sanrio Co., Ltd.

 *Harmony Land*

"Will Put a Smile on Your Face and Love In Your Heart"

Located in the town of Hiji in Oita Prefecture, where it is said that a magical White Bird descended to earth to bring happiness to all. The outdoor theme park takes full advantage of the natural setting. Daily parades and live shows with Kitty and other Sanrio characters create a vibrant amusement park. Check out Kitty's castle that was remodeled especially for her 30th birthday! *Kitty's Tip*~ Strollers are allowed at this location. You can rent one for ¥300 at Guest Information.

Access

Take the JR Nippo Main Line from Kokura Sta. heading for Oita to Kitsuki Station. Or take the JR Nippo Main Line from Oita Sta. heading for Beppu to the Hiji Station. *Kitty's Tip* ~ The first route will take seventy minutes, whereas the second route only takes thirty minutes. It is not possible to walk to the park from either station, instead you will have to take a taxi or the local bus.

Admission

Adult ¥3,800, Youth ¥3,200 and Child ¥2,800. This entrance fee includes all attractions. There are different types of tickets, which give limited access to events and these are best checked out online at <http://www.sanrio.co.jp/english/harmony/ hl_guide/hl_ticket.html>. *Kitty's Tip* ~ Sometimes special discount coupons are offered on the official site. Always check there first before heading out!

Location

Fujiwara 5933, Oaza Hijimachi
Hayami-gun, Oita-ken (on Route 10)
Tel: 0977-73-1111
The official Harmonyland Japanese website:
http://www.sanrio.co.jp/harmony/welcome.html
The official Harmonyland site in English:
http://www.sanrio.co.jp/english/harmony/harmony.html

Hours Of Operation

The park opens daily from 9AM to 5PM. It is best to check with the main website as hours of operation may change. The park is closed the 2nd & 3rd Wednesdays and Thursdays of every month.

Services

An information house is conveniently located near the entrance gates. Here you can rent strollers, buy extra film, a disposable camera, or even send your Harmonyland postcards. *Kitty's Tip* ~ If you happen to be at the park on your birthday, a free souvenir birthday present is available from the information house.

Attractions

Sanrio Character Boat Ride ~ Enter the enchanted land of Sanrio characters. Detailed sets and thematic music sweep you into this fantasyland.

Kitty Castle ~ A tour of the castle ends with the chance to take a picture with Kitty. For her birthday she held up a sign that said "My Happy Birthday."

Character Ferris wheel ~ Enjoy a 15 minute ride high atop Harmonyland. Each gondola is a different character on this multicoloured Ferris wheel.

Harmonyland Theatre ~ A variety of musicals are showcased here.

Harmony Train ~ Catch the train and see some of the breathtaking Oita landscape while you journey from Harmony Park Station to Carnival Square.

Fairy Carousel ~ A beautiful two tiered merry-go-round with magnificent white ponies.

Pop n' Smile ~ Cute character gondolas take you on a ride.

Courtesy of Sanrio Co., Ltd.

Chapter Twenty-Five
Kitty Quiz 🌸

Kitty Quotes ~ "Everyone Is Part Of The Show—Just Bring Your Imagination" 2000

Kitty's ever-evolving designs have always incorporated her positive outlook on life, her thoughts on friendship and family, and even style. Through the amazing array of products created over the past thirty years, Kitty has evolved into a rich character.

Do you consider Kitty to be one of your best friends? Would she always be on your speed dial, her birthday programmed into your BlackBerry®, or a place set for her at the table? If so, ask yourself this—how well do you know Kitty?

Test out your knowledge below!

(Q1) Can you name at least three things which Kitty likes?
(A) Hot milk, drawing, TV, cake, apples, riding her tricycle, and visiting her Uncle's farm, among many other things. *Source: bag 1976*

(Q2) What does Mama White like to bake?
(A) Cakes, apple pies, and cookies. *Source: apron 1976*

(Q3) How much did it cost Kitty to ride on the elephant at the amusement park?
(A) 50 cents. *Source: notebook 1979*

(Q4) What is Kitty's favourite item?
(A) Her red ribbon. *Source: standing mirror 1977*

(Q5) What is the most relaxing time of day?
(A) Tea time, of course. *Source: notebook 1984*

(Q6) What is Kitty's favourite kind of party?
(A) A tea party. *Source: hand soap 1990*

(Q7) What is Kitty's favourite toy?
(A) Just too many to choose from! *Source: Kitty*

(Q8) What are the five wee wonders of the world?
(A) A big tree, a little bird, a toy train, nice apples, and Hello Kitty. *Source: handy case 1977*

(Q9) With whom does Kitty share her umbrella?
(A) Tiny Chum. *Source: drawstring bag 1988*

(Q10) Where was Kitty's first holiday abroad?
(A) She went on vacation to an island in the South Seas. *Source: vinyl carrier 1980*

(Q11) What is the first sport Kitty is seen playing?
(A) Tennis. *Source: lunch cup 1980*

(Q12) How many sisters or brothers does Kitty have?
(A) One sister, Mimi. *Source: handkerchief 1975*

(Q13) What brightens Kitty's day?
(A) Hearts and flowers. *Source: pencil case 1992*

(Q14) What treats await Kitty at Grandma's house?
(A) Apples and cookies. *Source: knapsack 1991*

(Q15) Who does Kitty think is tops?
(A) Tiny Chum. *Source: pencil lead case 1990*

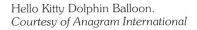

Hello Kitty Dolphin Balloon.
Courtesy of Anagram International

(Q16) Which American state did Kitty visit in 1988?
(A) Florida. *Source: vinyl bag 1988*

(Q17) What is Kitty's favourite drink in the summer?
(A) A nice cold soda. *Source: nametag 1989*

(Q18) What is Kitty's room full of?
(A) Fun and play. *Source: mini album 1975*

(Q19) What instrument did Kitty play when she went to the circus?
(A) A trumpet, and she was accompanied by an elephant on drums. *Source: 1987 pencil case*

(Q20) What are Kitty's grandparents' names?
(A) Anthony and Margaret White. *Source: letterset 1979*

(Q26) What color was Kitty's first rotary phone?
(A) Red. *Source: mini scale set 1976*

(Q) Can you name three toys in Kitty's room?
(A) Crayons, a wagon, ring toss and a ball, etc. *Source: mini album 1975*

(Q27) When did Kitty first pilot a plane?
(A) 1978. *Source: Go Skyward! Case 1978*

(Q28) What three colors were used for Kitty's bow in the 1970s?
(A) Red, blue, and yellow were all used.

(Q29) What string instrument does Kitty play?
(A) The violin. *Source: notebook 1978*

(Q30) What does Kitty like to do on nice days?
(A) Ride her tricycle with Mimi. *Source: thermos 1977*

Wow! Look at how much you know about Kitty!! Look over some of your special Kitty items to see how much more there is to learn about your favourite little white kitten. **Happy Tails!**

Chapter Twenty-Six

How Much Is That Kitty In The Window?

Kitty Quotes ~ "When The Sun Smiles I Perk Up My Whiskers & Smile Along With It" 1979

Hello Kitty goods have increasingly caught the eye of more and more collectors. Focusing perhaps on a particular design, production year or product, Hello Kitty collections are as varied as the people who love her.

In both Japan and North America there is a huge interest in items from the late 1970s, especially 1976. Looking at the use of primary colors, stencilled lettering, and Kitty's 'classic' poses makes it easy to see the attraction to the '70s. The designs still feel fresh today.

In the 1997 book *My Kitty*, Sanrio conducted a survey of second-hand stores in Tokyo and came up with an average value for select items. Jewelry, paper items, and small figurines from the 1970s to early '80s were up a third. Rare and much sought after items such as the Sanrio 30th birthday television almost doubled in price. The first product, the petite purse priced at $2 U.S. in 1976 was valued at $41 U.S. in 1997. It would be closer to $82 U.S. in today's market.

The biggest change in values since Sanrio did this survey almost eight years ago has been the surge of interest in the 1980s. The '80s items are still not commanding the prices of those from the '70s, but for rare items such as the Hello Kitty rotary phone they are quickly increasing. If you are a fan of the tartan or still photography series, then this is the decade for you.

The 1990s to the present has seen the least amount of change in price. Limited releases or unique items would garner the most interest.

Prices given in this book are for items which are in mint condition. If an item is worn or damaged then the value is diminished. Values are meant as a guide to the reader. Neither the author nor the publisher assumes responsibility for any losses that may be incurred as a result of consulting this book.

Buy only what pleases you and keep that Sanrio motto inside your head at all times "Small gift big smile." Happy Collecting!

Thanks to the internet Hello Kitty's world is getting even smaller. From games and crafts to online shopping and chatting, the complete Hello Kitty® experience is available at the touch of a paw. **Welcome!**

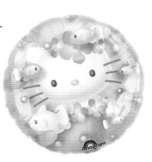

 In The Loop

Hello Kitty 's Official Site ~ Friends can keep up to date with all her fantastic activities.

http://www.sanrio.com/hellokitty/

Hello Kitty 30 Years ~ This official Japanese site shows an amazing range of Hello Kitty creations spanning her thirty years. Click on a star to see products from your favorite production year. **Simply incredible!**

http://kitty30.com/main.html

Sanrio Official Site ~ For the complete Sanrio experience check out this site. Major categories include store, what's new, go shop, etc.

http://www.sanrio.com/

Sanrio Japan Official site ~ Yes, of course it is entirely in Japanese but worth looking at for the pictures alone.

http://www.sanrio.co.jp/welcome.html

Sanrio Japan English Page ~ A brief overview of the company and international store locations are given. There are also write-ups on Hello Kitty's family, friends, design history and a quiz.

http://www.sanrio.co.jp/english/

Sanrio Town ~ You must become a member first but once you sign in you are able to have your own Hello Kitty email address, play games, contribute to the online community board, etc. The site is multilingual: Japanese, English, Chinese and Korean.

http://www.sanriotown.com/

 Let's Play!

The Sanrio site has many downloadable and interactive games. There is something for everyone including coloring pages and fun psychological tests. Perhaps a Hello Kitty Trivial Pursuit™ game is not far behind?

Official Sites

Sanrio On-Line Games ~ Hello Kitty Shapes & Colors game.

http://www.sanrio.co.jp/english/multimedia/s_gallery/s_gallery.html

Hello Kitty Psychological Test ~ On the official Sanrio site an amusing game can be found.

http://www.sanriotown.com/psycho/psycho6/psycho6_us.htm

Sanrio Official Know It All Quiz ~ Five fun questions test your knowledge of Hello Kitty.

http://www.sanrio.co.jp/english/characters/kt_quiz/ktquiz00.html

Hello Kitty Goods Picture Test ~ Answer the **yes** or **no** questions and be led through a maze in order to determine what kind of a friend you are. A good one to be sure!

http://www.sanriotown.com/psycho/psycho.htm

Above:
Hello Kitty Mermaid Balloon. *Courtesy of Anagram International*

A Fortune Corner ~ Click to discover what amazing things await you in the New Year.

http://www.sanrio.co.jp/english/fortune/fortune.html

Hello Kitty's Puzzle Game ~ Put together the scrambled twenty-four piece puzzle to see Hello Kitty's home.

http://www.sanrio.co.jp/english/multimedia/s_gallery/kioku_demo.html

 We Love You To Pieces!

Hello Kitty Printables & Crafts have never looked so cute! From official to private sites, there are many opportunities for fans to make unique Hello Kitty creations.

Sanrio's Official Site ~ There are lots of printouts for the young Hello Kitty fan and a 'Made by Mimmy' section. Cute craft ideas include a Hello Kitty doll made from recycled materials around the house. The craft archive will keep you busy! Crafts include CD covers, door hangers, and mini Halloween bags.

http://www.sanrio.com/main/games/kittyhouse/kittymain/kittyshouse.html

Hello Kitty Club ~ The official Japanese Sanrio site for members only. The page is in Japanese but definitely worth a visit.

http://www.hellokitty.ne.jp/

Dltk's Printable Crafts For Kids ~ A child-friendly site with many coloring templates and ideas. Hello Kitty coloring sheets, paper crafts, cross stitch patterns, iron on t-shirt transfers, and pumpkin carving patterns to name just a few.

http://www.dltk-kids.com/crafts/cartoons/hellokitty/index.htm

Dltk's Printable Crafts For Kids ~ Hello Kitty On-Line jigsaw puzzles ~ Hello Kitty as an Angel, Fairy, with Flowers, Flower Fairy, and Mermaid.

http://www.dltk-kids.com/crafts/cartoons/hellokitty/puzzles.htm

Pin the Bow on Hello Kitty ~ A variation of the pin the tail on the donkey game.

http://www.dltk-kids.com/crafts/cartoons/hellokitty/game.htm

Hello Kitty Cake ~ Make your birthday extra special with this idea to design your own Hello Kitty inspired cake. **Yum!**

http://www.dltk-kids.com/crafts/cartoons/hellokitty/cake.htm

 Shall We Shop?

No matter where you live, finding the perfect Hello Kitty item is easy through online shopping and Sanrio's worldwide stores. With over 600 new items released monthly, the shopping couldn't be better.

Sanrio Store ~ Split into major categories including store, what's new, play games and go shop. Currently they only deliver to the United States, Canada, US Territories, and US Military Bases.

http://www.sanrio.com/

Sanrio Online Shopping Japanese Site ~ A very detailed site filled with the latest goods. Shipping is available only to a Japanese address.

http://www.sanrioworld.ne.jp/sanrio/

The World-Wide Shop List ~ To visit an actual Sanrio store please see the following link for addresses.

http://www.sanrio.co.jp/english/about_s/shoplist/shoplist.html

 Say Hello To Me

"The best part of my day is getting mail from my friends" says Hello Kitty . Keeping in touch with friends is easy and fun with e-cards. Check out these links to view super cute cards with Hello Kitty and a variety of other great Sanrio characters.

American Greetings™

http://www1.americangreetings.com/category.pd?path=46456&

Yahooligans® Sanrio e-cards

http://yahooligans.yahoo.com/content/ecards/category?g=28

Chapter Twenty-Eight

Kitty Stylish Goods ✿

Kitty Quotes ~ "Good Times 'R For Sharing With Friends" 1984

 Kitty Collections

Alexandre Herchovitch ~ http://www2.uol.com.br/herchcovitch/

Anagram® International, Inc. ~ http://www.anagramintl.com/

Bandai® America ~ http://www.bandai.com/

BDL/ Business Design Laboratory Co., Ltd. ~
        http://www.business-design.co.jp/en/

Blue Box Toys™ ~ http://www.blueboxtoys.com/

Brunswick® Bowling ~ http://www.brunswickbowling.com/

Casa D'Oro® ~ http://www.italiangoldcharms.com/

Fantas-Eyes ~ http://www.fantas-eyes.com/

Giddy Up, LLC. ~ http://www.giddyup.com/

High ItenCity® ~ http://www.highintencity.com/homepage.html

Jakks Pacific Inc. ~ http://www.jakkspacific.com/

KidKraft® ~ http://www.kidkraftinc.com/

Lambs & Ivy® ~ http://www.lambsandivy.com

MZ Berger & Company ~ http://www.mzberger.com/

Nakajima® USA, Inc. ~ http://www.nakajimausa.com/

Paul Frank Industries Inc. ~ http://www.paulfrank.com/

Peoples Revolution ~ www.peoplesrevolution.com

PEZ® Candy Inc. ~ http://www.pez.com/

Rayovac® ~ http://www.rayovac.com/

Rubik's® ~ http://dev.rubiks.com/index.cfm

Sababa Toys™ ~ http://www.sababatoys.com/

Sanrio Company Ltd. ~ http://www.sanrio.com/

Sanyo™ ~ http://www.sanyo.com/home.cfm

Spectra® Merchandising International, Inc. ~
        http://www.spectraintl.com/

Takara® USA Corp. ~ http://www.takara-usa.com/

The Tin Box Company ~ http://www.tinboxco.com/

Tomy® Dream Energy/Tomy Corporation ~ http://www.tomy.com/

Yamaha™ Motor Co. Ltd. ~ http://www.yamaha-motor.co.jp/
global/link/index.html

 Hello Kitty Charity Auction

Airstream™ Inc. ~ http://www.airstream.com/

BCBG Max Azaria ~ http://www.bcbg.com/

Betsey Johnson ~ http://www.betseyohnson.com/

Ernie Ball® ~ http://www.ernieball.com/

Esteban Cortazar ~ http://www.estebancortazar.com/

Eugenia Kim ~ http://www.eugeniakim.com/

Heatherette ~ http://www.heatherette.com/

Kimora Lee Simons ~ http://www.babyphat.com/

McKinnon Shapes & Designs ~ http://www.mckinnon-surf.com/

Michael Graves ~ http://www.michaelgraves.com/

Mossimo® Giannulli ~ http://www.mossimo.com/

Nirve® Sports Limited ~ http://www.nirve.com/main/

NYC PEACH ~ http://www.nycpeach.com/

Richard Walker ~ http://www.blinde.com/

Sonia Kashuk ~ http://www.soniakashuk.com/

Sheri Bodell ~ http://www.sheribodell.com/

Steve Madden ~ http://www.stevemadden.com/

Tarina Tarantino ~ http://www.tarinatarantino.com/

Tiffany Dubin ~ No current site

 Kitty Ex. Brand Collaboration

A Mon Avis ~ http://www.amonavis.jp/

CA4L4 ~ http://www.ca4la.com/

Garcia Marquez ~ http://www.garcia-style.com/

Hackford & Song ~ http://www.hackfordandsong.jp/

H.A.K ~ No current site

Hanway ~ http://www.hanway.jp/

Head Porter ~ No current site

Honey Salon ~ No current site

Lil'limo ~ http://www.lil-limo.com/

Loree Rodkin ~ http://www.loreerodkin.com/

Samantha Thavasa Japan Ltd. ~ http://www.samantha.co.jp/

White Trash Charms Japan ~ http://www.whitetrashcharms.com/

Chapter Twenty-Nine

Kitty Glossary ✿

Kitty Quotes ~ "Let's Be Friends" 2004

Byakkotai ~ The White Tiger Brigade of Aizu-Wakamatsu composed of fifteen or sixteen year old youths.

Daimonjiyaki ~ A great bonfire held on a hill in Kyoto every August 16th. Traditionally, bonfires were made to send off the ancestral spirits to the other world.

dango ~ A dumpling made of rice or wheat flour.

Edo ~ A period in Japanese history from 1603-1867.

geta ~ Raised wooden clogs with a thong-like strap.

gyoza ~ Japanese style dumplings.

hagoita ~ A wooden paddle used in a traditional New Years game.

hane ~ A shuttle.

hanetsuki ~ A traditional Japanese New Year's game played with a wooden paddle. The game is similar to badminton.

hanko ~ A name seal used in Japan instead of a signature.

Hina Matsuri ~ Doll Festival or Girl's Festival celebrated on March 3rd of each year. A daughter's happiness and success are celebrated on this day.

hiragana ~ A Japanese writing system.

kabuki ~ One of Japan's theatrical arts dating back to the Edo period.

kanji ~ Chinese characters, each with its own meaning and corresponding to a word.

katakana ~ A Japanese writing system based on syllables. It is mainly used for writing foreign words.

Kinkakuji ~ The Golden Pavilion Temple in Kyoto.

makoto ~ Sincerity.

manga ~ A graphic novel.

manju ~ A confectionary made of flour, rice powder, and buckwheat on the outside and filled with bean jam. There are different varieties.

mochi ~ A chewy rice cake eaten year 'round and a traditional New Years food.

ningyo ~ A doll.

ningyoaki ~ A small cake filled with bean paste.

noren ~ A traditional Japanese split curtain.

omamori ~ A Japanese good-luck charm. The word translates as protection. Many temples and shrines sell these.

sakura ~ Cherry blossom.

Shichigosan ~ A special celebration held on November 15th for all children turning 3, 5, or 7.

Shinsengumi ~ A group of private guards loyal to the Emperor, assembled at the end of the Tokugawa regime.

Shinto ~ The indigenous religion of Japan.

Tairyo ~ A large catch of fish.

The Strawberry News ~ The official monthly guide to Sanrio products. The official Japanese site is: http://www.sanrio.co.jp/characters/strawberry/strawberry.html

Toji ~ A Buddhist temple in Kyoto, recognized as a World Heritage Site. The name translates as East Temple.

Tokkaido ~ An extremely important route during the Tokugawa-era linking Tokyo to Kyoto.

Tsurugajo ~ A traditional fortress in Northern Japan.

yukata ~ A Japanese summer cotton kimono.

yuki mino ~ A traditional winter costume worn long ago in northern Japan.

Chapter Thirty
Kitty Bibliography

Kitty Quotes ~ "Always There When You Need A Helping Hand" 1997

 ## Books

Belson, Ken and Bremner, Brian. "Hello Kitty, The Remarkable Story of Sanrio and The Billion Dollar Feline Phenomenon." John Wiley & Sons PTE Ltd., 2004.

"Hello Kitty no Tezukuri Komono-Oshare de Cute na Kitty ga Ippa:Lady Boutique Series 1240." Boutique-sha, 1998.

"Hello Kitty Collection Cho Himitsu Get!." Popula sha, 2003.

"Kitty Ex. Perfect Guide Book." Bijutsu Co. Ltd., 2004.

"My Kitty." Asuka Shinsha, 1997.

Articles

Brian Bremner. "In Japan, Cute Conquers All," *Business Week Online*, 25 June 2002, <http://www.businessweek.com/bwdaily/dnflash/jun2002/nf20020625_7574.htm> (12 July 2004).

Brian Bremner. "Sanrio's Fabulous Feline Franchise," *Kateigaho International Edition*, Spring 2004, <http://www.kateigaho.com/int/mar04/hello-kitty.html> (4 August 2004).

Malika Browne. "Cool for Cats," *Times Online*, 27 November 2004, http://women.timesonline.co.uk/article/0,,17909-1374161,00.html. (1 December 2004).

Chisaki Watanabe. "Hello Kitty Still Purring After 30 Years,' *The Toronto Star*, 18 September 2004.

Coury Turczyn. "What Is This Thing Called Hello Kitty?" *PopCult*, 2003, <http://www.popcultmag.com/criticalmass/books/kitty/hellokitty1.html>. (5 September 2004).

David McMahon. "RPT- Feature-Hello Kitty Gets By With A Little Help From Friends," *Forbes*. 14 October 2003. <http://www.forbes.com/newswire/2003/10/14/rtr1108970.html> (12 August 2004).

"Doll Creates Consumer Frenzy in Japan," *The Lubbock Avalanche Journal Online,* 19 August 1999, <http://www.lubbockonline.com/stories/081999/bus_081999097.shtml> (12 August 2004).

Edward Gomez. "Asian Pop How Hello Kitty Came To Rule The World," *SF Gate,* 14 July 2004, <http://sfgate.com/cgi-bin/article.cgi?f=/g/a/2004/07/14/helkit.DTL> (20 August 2004).

Ed. "Hello Kitty, Way To Go!," *Japan Echo Inc.,* 2 April 2004, <http://web-japan.org/trends/fashion/fas040402.html> (7 August 2004).

"EU Hires Hello Kitty To Promote Friendship in Japan," *EU Business,* http://www.eubusiness.com/afp/040413045511.uzh3my4k/view (13 April 2004).

"Exhibition Celebrates 30 Years of Kitty-chan," *Daily Yomiuri*, (2004). <http://www.yomiuri.co.jp/newse/20040805woad.htm>.

Victoria Namkung. "Hello Kitty's Got A Brand New Bag," *Asian Week*, 21-27 September 2001, <http://www.asianweek.com/2001_09_21/biz_hellokitty.html> (1 December 2004).

Tomoko Otake. "The Cat's Whiskers Of Kawaii," *The Japan Times*, 24 October 2004, <http://www.japantimes.co.jp/cgi-bin/getarticle.pl5?fl20041024x1.htm> (29 November 2004).

Ginny Parker. "The Cult Of Cute," *Cnews*, 22 December 1999, <http://www.canoe.ca/CNEWSFeatures9912/22_cute.html> (4 August 2004).

"Hello Kitty Celebrates Thirtieth Anniversary," *What's Cool in Japan*, March 2004, <http://web-japan.org/kidsweb/cool/04-03/kitty.html> (6 August 2004).

"Hello Kitty At Thirty, Why We Love Her So," *Kateigaho International Edition*,(Spring 2004). < http://www.kateigaho.com/int/mar04/hello-kitty-30.html>.

"Hello, is Kitty there?," *The Toronto Sun*, AP 12 September 2004,

Kelly Carter. "Hello Kitty Is The Cat's Meow," *USA Today*, 21 April 2004, <http://www.usatoday.com/life/2002/2002-04-22-hello-kitty.htm> (4 July 2004).

Leo Lewis. "Hello Kitty Turns 30 and Keeps On Growing," *Japan Inc.*, September 2003, <http://www.japaninc.net/article.php?articleID=1177>.

Mary Roach. "Cute Inc.," *Wired Issue 7.12,* December 1999, <*http://www.wired.com/wired/archive/7.12/cute.html*> (20 August 2004).

"Nostalgia Fueling Hello Kitty's Return To Fashion," *The Los Angeles Times*. 10 February 2003, <http://www.tdn.com/articles/2003/02/10/this_day/news03.txt> (4 August 2004).

Parja Bhatnagar. "Hello Kitty's A Whisker Away From 30," *CNN Money*, 14 November 2003, <http://money.cnn.com/2003/11/14/news/companies/hello_kitty/> (5 august 2004).

"Puroland! The Magical Hello Kitty Theme Park," *The Happy Times*, July 2002, <http://www.sanrio.com/main/happytimes/feature/puroland.html>. (4 August 2004).

Websites

Sanrio Co. Ltd. Japanese Site (31 July 2004). <http://www.sanrio.co.jp/welcome.html>. (15 August 2004).

Sanrio Co. Ltd. USA Site (4 August 2004)< http://www.sanrio.com/>. (14 October 2004).

Sanrio Puroland (2004) <http://www.sanrio.co.jp/english/spl/spl.html>. (15 November 2004).

Harmonyland (2004) <http://www.sanrio.co.jp/english/harmony/harmony.html>. (16 November 2004).

Hello Kitty 30th Anniversary Site (2004) <http://kitty30.com/main.htm>l>. (11 September 2004).